1st edn

$6.00
$15

ROB3

LIVE
AT THE
VILLAGE
VANGUARD

LIVE
AT THE
VILLAGE
VANGUARD

Max Gordon

Introduction by
Nat Hentoff

St. Martin's Press
New York

Library of Congress Cataloging in Publication Data

Gordon, Max
Live at the Village Vanguard.

1. Village Vanguard (Nightclub)   2. Entertainers
——New York (City)   I.   Title.
PN1968.U5G6   792.7'09747'1   80-16041
ISBN 0-312-48879-3

To Rebecca,
Deborah,
Lorraine,
and to Sarah

Grateful acknowledgment is made to the following for their help in providing the photographs for this book: Robert Asen, Betty Comden, Frank Driggs, Frank Foster, Carol Friedman, William P. Gottlieb, Helen Keane, Harold Leventhal, Brian McMillen, Professor and Mrs. Archie Shepp, Mary Travers, and Arnie Unterbach.

LIVE
AT THE
VILLAGE
VANGUARD

Introduction

by Nat Hentoff

Like other select companies of mortals, jazz musicians have their own demonology. Perhaps the evilest of spirits are critics, closely followed by nearly all booking agents and most record company officials. But a special circle in this Hades is reserved for night club owners. Critics are invincibly ignorant; bookers are incurable liars; and recording executives never show you a true set of figures. But night club owners, so the lore goes, have *all* these pernicious characteristics—and besides, haven't the slightest interest in what the music's all about.

Or, as a number of musicians have said of some of these innkeepers—glaring at them in the long hours of early morning—"The bastard should be running a butcher shop."

Yet the night club owner, as musicians well know, is *the* vital element in the economic gestalt for musicians on the way up and for those who have gone out of fashion and want, as the times change again, one more shot at the moon. It is the club that provides the exposure that can lead to recording contracts, critical attention, and bookings at colleges, festivals and in attractive foreign climes. Maybe the owner should be running a butcher shop, but from where he *is*, he has a lot of power to change lives. One way or another. Another reason he is not beloved.

As in all things, there are exceptions. For more than thirty-five years, I have been writing about musicians and, perforce, about the clubs that give them sustenance. In all that nocturnal time, I

1

have not heard a single malign word from a performer about Max Gordon, whose Village Vanguard is the closest we have to the Camelot of jazz rooms. Not that he has hosted only jazz, of course, as these memoirs attest. But for a long time, the Vanguard has especially kept the jazz faith during parched years when Max could have made a whole lot more bread by putting in extra electrical outlets and then plugging in a series of interchangeable rock acts.

Musicians know about Max keeping the faith. Musicians all over the world. He actually stayed with the music he respected and even sometimes liked rather than cash in on current scams. That's more than some jazz musicians themselves have done—as witnessed by various "fusion" and "crossover" contortionists. A club owner who cares more about the music than some of the musicians! So now you know why Max is a kind of a legend among musicians and those of us who need—and I mean need—their music.

I do not mean, however, that Max is sentimentalized or idealized as he nears swinging beatification. It is also known that Max survives because he knows how to run a business. So he is no Midas to musicians. And while he is not a Teutonic administrator, he expects everyone to make time and take care of *their* business on the stand. So he is not the A. S. Neill of jazz club owners.

On the other hand, there is indeed more to Max than business. Much more. I have known him since I first came to New York in 1953. What most struck me about him then—and still does—was his lively sense of wonder. Of curiosity. As you can tell from this book, Max has always had, as they used to say, big ears. Big and open. He'll listen to just about anything, even if it's outside his experience. And he'll really *listen*—with expectancy. Much of it he won't buy, but at least he hasn't shut out any sounds automatically.

That openness is rare. It's rare among critics, even among musicians. And Max has another dimension that is even more rare. He may not like a particular way of music, but he is able to sense why it's valuable, why it needs a forum, why it needs the Vanguard. After all, Max is too genuinely hip to limit his interests to only that music and those performances that he himself can immediately dig. It's that curiosity of his again. And it includes

people who don't make music as well as those who do. As in the
reverberating sketches in this book of the vintage Village poets,
the jazz Baroness, and a good many other habitués of the Village
Vanguard.

Max's quick perceptiveness in the pursuit of his curiosity is the
source of this book's energy. Swiftly, but indelibly, he has caught
some of the basic chord changes in the dynamics of Charles
Mingus, Lenny Bruce, Miles Davis, Joe Glaser, Sonny Rollins,
Rahsaan Roland Kirk, et al. A good many so-called professional
writers have not done nearly so well, though they've used many
more words. The thing is Max knows how to listen, and how to
watch while he's listening. And one other thing. He can write.
And I don't think he learned that in Reed College all those
decades ago. I don't think anybody ever learned how to write in a
school. That skill comes, if it comes at all, with learning how to
feel a beat, and then how to ride it. Like in jazz. Indeed, my
theory of the literary flowering of Max Gordon is that its roots are
in all his years of listening to jazz. And to the wondrously diverse
speech of its makers. Coming up against all these stubbornly
individualistic voices during half a century or so, Max found his
own.

Anyway, however Max emerged as a writer, he has created
here a singular chronicle in the annals of urban (and sometimes
urbane) life after dark. Musicians and other performers have
detailed their odysseys—with themselves at center stage, of
course. And there have been impressionistic accounts of certain
streets and districts of historic importance in entertainment
history. But this is the first long-range view of one vital and
influential room by someone who saw it all—every night of its
existence.

And as you see and hear, in each chapter, how that one room
was able to encompass such extraordinarily variegated children of
the night—from Leadbelly to Lenny Bruce to Sonny Rollins—
you finally understand what Max means when he says that a place
takes on a life of its own. And that its owner had better pay
attention to the changing rhythms and needs of that place, or it'll
go cold.

That's why most night clubs go dark, sooner rather than later.
The owners stopped listening, or maybe never knew how to
listen beyond the cash register. They'd accept the hype of

booking agents and disc jockeys or see what was on the trade magazine charts that they could afford. But they had no inner voice. Or inner ear.

The clubs that do make it over long periods of time are those you fall into even when you're not sure who's there that night. You figure that it's not going to be a pretentious stiff or some two-chord superstar whose main blues influence seems to have been Henry Kissinger or his agent. In sum, you trust whoever runs the joint to have enough self-respect to have booked a performer with class. From what I've seen, that quality of faith in a club is evidenced more often at the Village Vanguard than at any other room I've ever known. And this trust goes farther. You may look in the paper to see who's playing, and the name doesn't mean much—if anything. But since it's the Vanguard, it's worth a shot.

To have created that degree of credibility—and to have sustained it so long—is quite an astonishing feat. And there are some students of either popular culture or indigenous American classical music (as Max Roach calls jazz) who have made pilgrimages to 178 Seventh Avenue South in Greenwich Village to witness, close up, the very repository of taste and acumen who is responsible for the Village Vanguard's resplendent longevity.

Each, in turn, descends the steep stairs and finds, near the entrance or in his fabled office in the kitchen, a short, slight, somewhat stooped soft-voiced man with a knowing eye and what at first seems a laconic approach to conversation. But if the talk—that is, the talker—interests him, the Founding Father opens up and reveals, in addition to the resonance of earned experience that courses through this book, considerable warmth. Which is also in this book.

Max, though essentially shy, likes people. All kinds. A rather necessary requirement for an innkeeper, especially one in Greenwich Village where "all kinds" encompasses more variety than can even be imagined in most other parts of the country, or the world. And, as in music, the diversity of his customers doesn't throw Max. Quite the opposite. The unpredictability of what comes down those stairs every night is one of the things that keeps him intrigued with his particular line of work.

In sum, it came to Max Gordon—as it comes to few people—that he found a true vocation rather early in his life. And he had the sense and sensibility to know it, and to nurture it. He has been a catalyst by which thousands upon thousands have known resoundingly memorable evenings of music and mordant comedy on his premises. And he's enjoyed himself too—for more nights than it took Scheherazade to tell her life-extending tales. Not a bad life. Not a bad life at all.

And by being himself, by being his own rhythm section and ignoring trendiness, Max has ultimately attracted listeners across generational lines. He didn't go after the young. He figured that, in time, some would feel themselves compelled to go down those stairs because what they had been hearing on the radio and in the discos and wherever else was just not satisfying enough. Not challenging. Actually, kind of dumb.

One night, some years ago, when there was still some obtuse talk about jazz being "dead" because rock had utterly drowned it, I started to walk to the Vanguard to hear Max Roach, as uncompromising a musician as Max Gordon is a club owner. I figured there'd be no problem getting in. It was past midnight; Max Roach does not appear on any of the "crossover" charts. And jazz was "dead," right?

There was a line. A line that went all the way around a long block. Older folks, as well as people in their thirties and twenties. And quite a few teenagers. Black, white, Asian, whatever. I felt so good, seeing that line, that if I'd had the bread, I would have bought them each a drink. In celebration of continuity.

Downstairs, Max Gordon was listening to the music while also, of course, keeping an eye on the place. He appears to have several eyes. And one of them kept looking up at the crowded staircase full of people eager to get inside the small, smoky, pulsing room. Not because it was chic to be there. But because serious people—often festively, seriously witty—were saying things from that stand that they had to say, whether there was an audience up front or not. You could feel their passion moving out into the room, and as the set went on, you might discover more of your own submerged emotions than you thought were there.

It is a special room that has lasted so long because of passion. That of its performers, and that of the watchful man, looking up the stairs to welcome, in his understated way, each new evening's voyagers into the light of improvisation.

Prologue

My mother brought us to New York in 1908—me, my brother, and two sisters—to Ellis Island from Lithuania, where I was born, to join my father, who had immigrated to America some years before to build a home in the promised land. My father settled in Providence, Rhode Island, rented a horse and wagon, and set out peddling eggs, butter, cheese, herring, house to house. By the time we arrived, he owned a store, with rooms in back of the store for us to move into.

Meanwhile a cousin from the same *shtetl* near Vilna where we came from was writing glowing letters to my father from Oregon, of the great economic opportunities out west. So in 1911 my father left his store in Providence, which was ailing, in charge of my mother, sat up four days and four nights in a train, and arrived in Portland, Oregon.

With the help of his cousin, my father started out again with a horse and wagon. He'd ride out into the adjacent farms and into the mountains of eastern Oregon, where hunters and trappers lived, and buy up raw hides and furs, which he'd bring back to Portland for shipment to St. Louis, Missouri. Once he saved up enough money, he turned in his horse and wagon for a Ford truck. He learned to drive it and sent five train tickets to Providence for us to join him.

I grew up in Portland, Oregon. Went to grammar school, high school, and to Reed College, where I graduated in 1924. My father didn't find gold at the end of the rainbow out west in Oregon, driving his Ford truck. We kids had to get out and hustle. I sold papers on the streets of Portland up to the day I graduated from Reed. My sisters graduated from high school and went to work to help pay the rent so my brother and I, "the boys in the family," could go to college.

There I was, fresh out of Reed College, with a major in literature. My father and mother wanted to know what I was going to do with myself now that I'd graduated. *They* knew what I should do—study to be a lawyer. They wanted a lawyer in the family. I didn't want to be a lawyer. I didn't know what I wanted to be, but I didn't want to be a lawyer.

"What's the matter, law isn't good enough for you?"

I thought law a predatory profession. Now you know what was eating me.

My brother was no problem. He knew what he wanted to be. My father and mother told him. They helped him pack and he left Portland for Cincinnati, Ohio, to study to be a rabbi, thank God, like they wanted him to. He was no trouble.

I had taken a course in creative writing at Reed College one semester, which I never got over. How could I tell my father and mother that? I didn't want to alarm them with strange, fancy notions about what I'd like to do with myself.

My father and mother didn't give up. "You'll go down the drain if you don't straighten yourself out. That's what'll happen to you," my mother said to me one day in the kitchen. "Go, go to New York if that's where you want to go. When you get there, you'll find a part-time job, do you hear? You'll have to. And you'll register at Columbia Law School. Once you're in, you'll change your mind about law."

So in 1926 I arrived in New York, found a job teaching English to immigrants, and went through the motions of matriculating at Columbia Law School. I lasted six weeks. I moved out of Livingston Hall on the Columbia campus and took the subway to Greenwich Village, where I'd been headed ever since I first set foot in New York.

Little did I know when I landed in the Village that I'd end up opening a nightclub, a joint in the Village. I'd never been to a nightclub. I didn't have any money, and I knew nothing about running one. Yet without any money, and with no experience, I stumbled into one of the toughest, most vulnerable businesses in the world. And here I am, nearly fifty years later, still at it, still running the same place: the Village Vanguard—open every night—the oldest nightclub in New York, they tell me.

An old customer of the Vanguard I hadn't seen for twenty

years dropped in one night. "I don't come here much anymore,"
was the first thing he said over a drink. "My son, my daughter
come here now. But I remember when I practically lived in this
joint. When I was going to N.Y.U., every Friday night—my
night out—where did I end up but at the Village Vanguard.
Yessir!"

"I read about this place—I read where *New Yorker* magazine
calls you 'the most prestigious jazz club in town.' What's
prestigious about it? I remember when Dyer-Bennet played a
lute here." He laughed.

"You don't like jazz?"

"My kids like it. You had folk music then: Leadbelly, Josh
White, Burl Ives, Pete Seeger. I was here the night Harry
Belafonte opened. What year was that? What year was it Judy
Holliday and those five kids worked here? She was seventeen at
the time."

"1940! Holy Jesus! How old *was* I then?"

"My kids tell me you don't have comedians here anymore.
Whatsamatter?"

"We got music, jazz music now."

"I know. I read it in the *New Yorker*."

"I remember Pearl Bailey here and 'the world's foremost
authority,' Irwin Corey, a funny guy. And Woody Allen and
Lenny Bruce. And you had some pretty good singers too: Dinah
Washington, Maxine Sullivan, Johnny Mathis. Whatever happened to Anita O'Day? Gone to California, eh, where the sun
never sets.

"My wife's probably wondering what the hell happened to me.
How 'bout another drink? The bar's closed? You're kidding. Hell,
I remember when you had no license. I brought my own bottle
and could pour myself a drink when I wanted it."

It was time to close, but he didn't want to go home. Nor did I.

"My kids tell me you wrote a book. Who wrote it?"

"I wrote it."

"You and who else?"

"I, I wrote it, mister."

"Don't get me wrong. I used to love this place, or I wouldn't
be talking to you like this. What's it about, this book?"

"The Village Vanguard, that's what it's about."

"What about The Blue Angel? And some of the other joints you
opened and closed in this town?"

"Opened and closed. Right. It's about that too, I guess."

"So you wrote a book. Where'd you find the time? My kids tell me you're here every night."

"Wrote it mornings before sun-up, longhand. Live at the Village Vanguard."

How come the Vanguard and I have survived? How did I happen to get into the nightclub business? This book is my answer to these persistent questions from customers, talent, and friends. Herein is a sampling of my adventures and encounters along the way, with some reflections on jazz, on what works in a nightclub, and on other matters. Some people seem surprised that the Vanguard *has* an owner. I know what they mean. Half the time I feel as though the place owns me.

1 : "You Don't Need Any Money"

Running a joint is tough, but my years in the Village before I opened one were tougher. I was living in a six-dollar-a-week room with a toilet in the hall, in the Strunsky block on West Third Street. Strunsky (I can still hear his asthmatic breathing as he climbed the stairs collecting rent) was a legendary Village landlord, the owner of a block of tenements bordered by Washington Square South and Sullivan, MacDougal, and West Third streets. He was the kind of landlord you could owe a week's rent to, two weeks', even a month's. A generation of Villagers owe their survival during the Depression to Strunsky.

I hung a suit on one of the wire hangers left over by the last tenant, put my secondhand typewriter on the floor, looked around and saw it was OK for sleeping. I didn't want to spend any more time in this room than I had to.

Stewart's Cafeteria on Sheridan Square was the reigning cafeteria of the day in the Village. You could always find somebody there who'd talk to you. So I slept all day and hung out at Stewart's all night.

Now that I was in the Village, what the hell was I gonna do with myself? I had to eat, pay the rent, and the few bucks in my pocket were fast running out. I'd have to do something, find something, some job at night preferably so that I could have my days to myself to look around, flex my ego, see what might turn up. It shouldn't be a job that'd tie me down, but a stopgap job until something right came along, though what that right job might be I had no idea.

My first job was in a loft on lower Fifth Avenue, a mail-order house where I was assigned the task of reading copy on sales

11

letters before they were "personalized" by an automatic type-writing process. I worked from six P.M. to two A.M. and hated every minute of it. At two A.M. I'd walk down to Stewart's Cafeteria and hang out till daylight.

I did this for a year. One night I decided I'd had it. So the next night I went to Grand Central, spent four days and four nights on a train, and landed home in Portland, Oregon. My father spoke to me without acrimony, and my mother cooked and baked to mark my homecoming. But I felt the cold draft of their worry and disapproval. Six months later I was back in the Village at a table in Stewart's Cafeteria.

I found a job in a one-man advertising establishment, helping the boss put together a catalogue for an electrical fixture firm on West Fourteenth Street. My job was to write brief, succinct descriptions of electrical gadgets. I was fired. Next, I walked off the street in answer to a sign in the window of a delicatessen in the fur district: Wanted, Counterman. I lasted ten minutes. I couldn't hold two cups in my left hand while working the coffee urn with my right. I could fill only one cup of coffee at a time, which wasn't enough for a busy delicatessen. I was no counter-man.

Months passed when I didn't look for a job. I didn't want a job; I could get by without a job.

If you were broke, the best place I knew of to be broke in was Greenwich Village. You could always bum a cigarette, a cup of coffee, even a bed for the night.

A Villager in one of his more candid moments once told me: "I walk in to Stewart's Cafeteria, grab a check, pick up a tray, walk over to the steam table, and I order the roast beef medium-rare with two vegetables. The counterman punches my check. I carry my tray over to a table, and I sit down. When I'm through eating, I sit, and I wait. I'm in no hurry. Some days I got to sit there longer than I like. It's a good thing Stewart's is open all night. It never fails but somebody I know will drop in, somebody who's got sixty cents, and bail me out."

When things got real tough, I'd assume the old routine, scanning the want ad columns of the morning papers: the *Times*, the *World*, the *Herald-Tribune*, for likely jobs. One day I spotted this ad:

Writer wanted for small magazine catering to Madison Ave. and the financial community. No experience necessary.

It sounded like the kind of job I was looking for. I got the job. It paid no salary. I worked on a commission basis.

I'd arrive about ten A.M. in the editorial room on Beekman Street. There was a staff of five, sometimes six; the number and composition changed daily. The boss editor, a tall, lean man, his face hooded in a green eye shade, was already there. He had searched the business and financial pages of the morning papers and was ready for us with small items, mostly personal, of what had happened overnight in the business and advertising community: A vice-president moved up to be president of a corporation; a fat account landed by an advertising agency; a creative lady executive now bossing men who once bossed her; an old product repackaged; a forward-looking operation involved in the takeover of another company; men assigned to foreign parts—all these items were ready for editorial treatment by the staff.

My job was to write a three-hundred-word congratulatory article, a puff, hailing the event that had overtaken the gentleman or lady I'd never heard of until that very morning.

Salesmen manning telephones in the next room lost no time in calling up the subject of the article brought in by "our investigative reporters" to read it for omissions and corrections. Said article was scheduled for next week's issue of the magazine, *The Commercial Reporter*. Would they care to have copies of the article reserved for them, their family, their friends? A hundred reprints, five hundred reprints, a thousand reprints? Cost: thirty-five cents a reprint, C.O.D. A messenger would deliver them pronto.

You'd be surprised how many fell for the pitch. I got twenty-five percent of the take. I worked there six months and never saw a published copy of *The Commercial Reporter*.

One night I met a girl named Ann at Stewart's Cafeteria. The next night I went down to Paul's Rendezvous on Wooster Street where she, dressed in pink pajamas, worked as a waitress for tips. Ann was a nice, blond, sassy girl with high cheekbones and a ready laugh. This was my first visit to Paul's.

I had never, in fact, been to a nightclub before. There weren't any in Portland that I knew of. During my undergraduate years at Reed, bolder students met in a clandestine apartment to drink the local gin. I remember the awful taste of that gin. I remember a girl holding her nose to swallow the stuff, get it down without spilling or heaving it. That was about the extent of my nightlife experience before I came to the Village.

Ann greeted me like an old friend, took me over to a booth where she was sitting with some friends or customers, I couldn't tell which, and introduced me. It was first-name Greenwich Village society, and I felt at home. She sat down next to me. Whenever her duties as a waitress called her, she got up, then came back and took her seat.

"This used to be a real Village joint when I first came to work here," she said. "But Paul's let the Bronx and Brooklyn move in and spoil the joint. He doesn't know it, but I'm quitting the first chance I get."

Here I was thinking how great Paul's was, and Ann was telling how awful it had become.

"That's John Rose Gildea, the poet," Ann whispered. It was the first time I'd ever seen a live poet. I knew of people who wrote poetry. We had them in Portland. But this was the first time I ever saw a poet who not only was a poet but looked like a poet—large head, long hair, eager eyes, shirt open at the throat. At the moment, John was pouring himself a drink of what looked like gin.

After that, I'd go to Paul's every night and hang around till closing time, four A.M., to walk Ann home. We'd walk down West Fourth Street to Hubert's Cafeteria, an all-night Village hangout where Ann knew everybody. I'd carry a couple of cups of coffee from the counter to a table, and we'd sit down.

"I shouldn't put my foot into this joint," Ann said to me one night. "Old man Hubert is a fink: Poor Joe Gould poured himself a bowlful of ketchup and mustard, so what does old man Hubert do? He has all the mustard and ketchup bottles removed from the tables. I really should boycott this joint."

"Who's Joe Gould?" I asked her.

"He's a poet who likes mustard and ketchup," Ann laughed. "I never see him at Paul's anymore. Paul won't let him in."

Ann had come to the Village from a farm in Wisconsin, with a stopover in Chicago, about two years before. She was a sturdy, self-confident girl. When she got here, she met a musician from Iowa who was studying classical piano and driving a cab at night. She moved in with him. Some months later, when she discovered that he had taken up with a man, she moved out. She wouldn't have moved out if it'd been another woman. She could cope with another woman, but a man was different.

So Ann moved into a furnished room that fronted on Washington Square, the more expensive side of the Strunsky block. Old man Strunsky let her have it because he knew her tips at Paul's could carry the fifteen-dollar weekly rental those rooms demanded.

When I had the money, I'd buy a bottle of home brew from a super on the block and carry it upright in a paper bag to Ann's room, careful not to disturb the yeast sediment at the bottom of the bottle.

Ann's room was always crowded with friends, neighbors, weekenders from Yale. I couldn't tell whether she'd never been to bed at all or was just getting up.

On her night off from Paul's, Ann and I'd make the rounds of the other Village joints: Romany Marie's, the Gypsy Tavern, the Black Cat. Ann hated all of them. Romany Marie was a snob; the two sisters in peasant costumes who ran the Gypsy Tavern were phony; the Black Cat was dark and full of menace. Then there was the Alimony Jail on West Fourth Street. Its high-backed booths were designed for necking and fornication. "Why don't they go home if that's what they want?" said Ann. The Fifth Circle on Varick Street was a laugh. The ex-rabbi who ran it featured seminars on sex, with questions from the floor: Should a woman propose marriage to a man? "Juvenile stuff," said Ann. "The last straw is what's become of Stewart's Cafeteria. They hired a bouncer, a goon with muscles to patrol the place. There isn't a decent place left in the Village," was her verdict.

"I'm quitting Paul's," Ann announced one day. "Because what do you think happened last night? Graham Norwell, a hell of an artist, came to the door 'bout two A.M., and Paul wouldn't let him in. True, Norwell was drunk and in his bare feet. He must've lost his shoes somewhere along the way. Well, Paul wouldn't let him in. Norwell painted Paul's murals four years ago for three bottles of gin. Paul doesn't remember that. He was glad to let him in then, when he needed him.

"The trouble with Paul is," Ann went on, "he's making too damn much money. He turned his joint over to a fast, hard-drinking crowd of uptown tourists who've got plenty of money to spend. So he doesn't have room for Villagers without money anymore—the same Villagers who made him, when he was getting started five years ago. That's Paul for you. I'm splitting. I won't work for a guy like that," said Ann with finality.

"Why don't we—you and me—open a straight-ahead place in

the Village?" said Ann. She was impulsive like that. "A real Village place! A no bullshit kind of place! I know everybody—all the poets: Max Bodenheim, John Gildea, Joe Gould, Eli Siegel, Bob Clairmont. They'd follow me wherever I go. It'd be terrific!"

"What do we use for money?" I asked her.

"You don't need any money to open a place in the Village," she said. "My friend Al, who likes the Bohemian atmosphere and lends money on the side—fifty bucks for sixty in return—he'll let us have a hundred. Al would like to have a stake in a Village rendezvous where he can meet girls. I know Al."

"What the hell do I know about running a Village place?"

"I'll run it. I'll show you the ropes."

I thought about it. I thought about it so hard that we opened the Village Fair on Sullivan Street in 1932. I didn't have any money except for the hundred I borrowed from Al. I didn't know what I was doing. But at first it didn't seem to matter.

I had dreamt of the kind of place I'd like to open in the Village: a quiet, gentle place, the kind of place where Sam Johnson hung out in eighteenth-century London. You dropped in, met your friends, heard the news of the day, read the daily papers provided by the house. When it got crowded at night, as I hoped it would, and the conversation soared and bristled with wit and good feeling, perhaps a resident poet would rise and declaim some verses he had composed for the entertainment and edification of the guests. That's the kind of place the Village Fair was going to be.

A week after it opened, Ann disappeared and left me holding the bag. I heard from her two years later. She was living in Miami with a textbook salesman.

In those days Prohibition was rife in the land. Customers brought their own bottles. The Village Fair served tea, coffee, sandwiches, and setups. Before I knew it, without anything I did or planned, the place assumed a dimension that took my breath away. Assorted weekend Villagers and out-of-towners discovered the Fair. They walked in with bottles in brown paper bags, ordered glasses and a bowl of ice, stared at the poets, at the "freaks," and at one another, and proceeded to get drunk, all for seventy-five cents minimum charge per person. It was cheap, handy, and the customers liked the "Bohemian atmosphere." It was no place for Dr. Johnson anymore.

During Prohibition, if you stepped out on the town for a night's entertainment, you carried a bottle with you. If you happened to forget it, or if your bottle ran dry at midnight, and you found yourself in some joint in the Village, where would you go to get another bottle?

There was always a guy in a doorway hanging outside Village joints who could get you one. You stepped outside, made the deal, went back inside, sat down and waited. Your waitress would tell you when your bottle had arrived. So you stepped outside again, passed the money to the messenger, picked up your bottle in a brown paper bag, and joined your party inside. The legal niceties were thus observed. The sale was made outside the premises and the joint was in the clear.

One night a guy in shirtsleeves who turned out to be a cop arrested me for selling him a bottle of gin. I didn't sell him a bottle of gin. I didn't have the muscle or know-how to sell booze in Prohibition New York. But this cop, acting in the line of duty, instead of going outside to complete the deal, pushed his money (larded with a massive tip) at the waitress and asked her would she please step to the door and bring him his bottle, like a good girl. That did it. The money was passed on the premises. Once an arrest was made, a cop in uniform was installed on the premises to see that the crime that hadn't happened wouldn't happen again. That's how it was done in those days. That finished the Village Fair.

Three months later when my case came up, I won a dismissal, but it was too late to save the Fair.

All was not over though because now I was in demand. I was a man with a following in the nightclub business, so Frankie Starch offered me a partnership in his West Third Street speakeasy that was ailing and empty. No cash investment. "Just come in and bring that crowd from the Village Fair with you." I could draw forty a week as a partner. Frankie had status in the neighborhood as the cousin of Tony Bender, the boss of Greenwich Village.

I didn't know what I was getting into. When I discovered Frankie kept a baseball bat in the back of the bar, I thought I'd better split, even though I had his place crowded inside of a week. After two months I proposed that he keep it all himself. He didn't like it, but I made it stick.

18 : Live at the Village Vanguard

So I was back where I started from, broke and unemployed, hanging out in Sheridan Square cafeterias, wondering when and if I'd ever get back into action again.

Without Harry the plumber I don't believe I ever would have.

2 : A Voice from the Basement

Not everyone I met in the cafeterias and other Village hangouts turned out to be an artist or a poet. Some plied more homely trades. Harry Simon, for instance, was a plumber and electrician. He could paint and plaster walls, fix leaks and stopped-up toilets, exterminate roaches. Villagers whose rooms needed such coarse domestic attention went out looking for Harry. They knew where to find him. Usually after midnight, he was at a back table in Hubert's Cafeteria.

Short, stocky, sooty, and in overalls, Harry was always just coming off a job at the Federation of Teachers union hall, the National Maritime Union offices, or Communist Party headquarters—places seemingly in constant need of repairs.

Harry had a friend, Barney, who owned a truck. If you were dispossessed and had to move your bed, chairs, books, and typewriter to more hospitable quarters, you knew where to find Barney. He was at the table with Harry. His truck was for hire if it wasn't laid up for repairs in some corner gas station.

What was important is, if you didn't have ready cash, Barney would wait for his money.

Barney's sister used to come down to the Village looking for him, afraid he was in some kind of trouble. Barney had spent a year in an upstate mental institution, and she was afraid he might, as once happened, suffer a relapse. "If people would only pay him what they owed him," she used to say, "I wouldn't have to worry about him so much."

In my walks around the Village, I found a basement on Charles Street that had once been run by Jack Delaney, the sign *Raided Premises* still nailed to the front door. It looked like a good

19

location for the place I had in mind. The landlord was glad to let me have it—no lease, no signed agreements; just pay fifty bucks, the first month's rent, and move in.

The first person I told about this was Harry, because I knew that I would need a man like Harry if I was ever going to get started in the nightclub business again. When I asked him would he work with me and would he wait for his money until after I got opened, he said: "Don't ask me to throw up jobs that put bread on my table, like my mother used to say."

"I'm giving you my word," I told him. "Keep a timecard. After I'm open I'll pay you every cent."

"What're you gonna call the place? Forget Village Fair. You're not gonna run a circus."

"It's a basement," I began.

"Call it The Subway then," said Harry. "No, that's not it. The Cellar. Nah, Underground, that's better. It means something."

"Underground." I tried it on for size. "It sounds kind of sneaky. I like a more open name," I said.

We kicked a few more names around, and then Harry came up with one: The Village Vanguard.

"I like it," I said.

It did something to Harry, my saying I liked it, that I liked the name "Vanguard."

"For a place called Vanguard," he said, "I'd be willing to wait for my money." That's the kind of guy Harry was.

It was agreed that Harry would wait for his money until the Vanguard opened, but I had to promise him I'd keep a little ready cash around to take care of spot deals and purchases he might find it necessary to make.

The first thing he did was buy two garbage cans. Then he found some empty ginger ale bottles in a corner of the basement, left over by Jack Delaney no doubt. He used them to kill the brown rats that infested the place. He had an uncanny and lethal aim. At first we worked by the light of plumber's candles he placed on the basement floor. Con Edison had demanded a seventy-five-dollar deposit. I didn't have seventy-five dollars, so Harry plugged into the meter feeding the hall lights of the tenements upstairs. Once we had some light, Harry could sweep the place. He discovered the sidewalk grating. A good place for the exhaust fan. "I know where I can pick one up for ten bucks," he said. "We'll need a ladder." I had enough money left to buy a ladder.

I knew I'd have to find some more money somewhere. I had a friend, Harold Weinstein, who was studying for his Ph.D. in history and Russian at Columbia. I took the subway to 116th Street to see him. When I told him what I needed a hundred bucks for, he said I was crazy, but he let me have it. He'd have to stint on his dinners, he said. (I've never paid back that hundred. Poor Harold went down in a ship, in 1938 or '39, part of a convoy on the way to Murmansk.)

Now that Harry had some money to work with, he found a four-burner gas stove in an empty apartment on Jane Street, paid the owner ten bucks and carried it down the steps of the emerging Vanguard on his back. Some Villager couldn't afford to keep his upright piano. Harry paid him twenty-five for it. Barney moved it for ten.

I found I could get credit in one paint and hardware store on Sullivan Street run by two brothers, sons of an Italian family that had immigrated to New York and settled in the Village.

The sons of Italian immigrants were living through their first Depression in America. Some went off to the government-run CCC camps. Their worried families got them off the street that way. Others hung around street corners and doorways, not knowing what to do with themselves. They'd run errands delivering bottles of booze for the "cordial shops" that pockmarked the Village. They'd hail you a cab for a tip. They stalked lone walkers down dark streets or rolled drunks asleep in Washington Square Park.

But there were some who opened stores, like the brothers on Sullivan Street, stayed home, and helped the folks with the rent and the groceries.

They gave me credit because I guess they were confident they'd get paid. They had "cousins" who helped them collect, two or three cousins who came around with the bill when it was due. They were courteous, didn't say much, would wait three days, a week, but I knew I'd better have it on the appointed day or else. So I hustled, got the money, and paid.

I learned one day that the Police Department licensed cabarets and that it cost fifty bucks a year. You filled out an application in triplicate, got three passport photos made, and took it all down to the station house where you were summarily fingerprinted. Not only that, but I was told that the poets would have to be fingerprinted too, if they wanted to recite their poetry at the Vanguard, or any singer off the street or itinerant tap dancer who might walk in and perform for quarters thrown at their feet. I'd have to keep their faces and fingerprints on file for any policeman who took it into his head to walk in and inspect the joint.

In addition to all that, a joint needed two exits and two johns in order to deserve a cabaret license. The Vanguard had only one exit and one john.

"To hell with a cabaret license," I said.

"Right," said Harry. "You ain't gonna run a cabaret, a line of girls with legs, a stand-up comic telling dirty jokes. That's entertainment. A poet shooting his mouth off is no entertainment."

I decided I'd open without a cabaret license. The Village Vanguard was beginning to take shape.

Harry's involvement in the growing Village Vanguard was becoming deeper every day. One night, after finishing the job plastering a wall, he said to me, "A good place for a mural. I know the girl to paint it, the greatest mural painter in New York. You can pay her after you open, like me. I'll call her up. This mural should be the center, the guts of the Vanguard!" he said.

Harry used to watch Kitty at work on the mural. He'd stop in the middle of whatever he was doing and stand there, fascinated. The theme of the mural was New York, the streets of New York, a scene evoking and celebrating New York. Kitty painted faces, bold, defiant, marching faces of workers bearing placards. While she was touching up the faces, Harry said, "Union Square! A demonstration in Union Square. It's beautiful!"

The night we opened Harry walked me over to the mural. Harry was cleanshaven and wearing a suit, the first time I'd seen him in a suit. He wanted me to see something. The mural was lit by two, hooded one-hundred-watt bulbs that Harry had installed. He stood before the mural, asked me if I saw anything special. I didn't see anything special among all those faces. I had watched Kitty working on the mural for a month.

"Look close," he said.

I looked close.

"Look closer, then look at me," he said. "You see that face?" he asked, smiling and pointing. "Look at it. Look at it good. That's me. Do you see it? It's me!"

I opened my eyes, and by God it was Harry. An unmistakable likeness of Harry among all of the faces in the mural.

"Don't get sore at Kitty. I talked her into it." He put his arm around my shoulder. "Promise me you won't say a word to Kitty."

I never did.

The mural was long finished; the cement floor painted a brick red; the upright piano was tuned and waiting in a corner. Harry found a small radio that would be useful for intermission. In fact, the Village Vanguard looked like it was ready to open for business, except for one thing. I had no chairs and no tables. I had scoured the Bowery for secondhand chairs and tables, but on the Bowery you had to put cash on the line and I had no money.

"Let's open without chairs and tables," said Harry. But I advised against it. "Let's wait. Something will turn up."

When I had the money, I used to eat the dollar-forty four-course table d'hote dinner in a little restaurant on Barrow Street called The White Whale, owned by a buxom maiden lady named Frances Bell. Summers she ran The White Whale in Province-town, Mass., and this year she had moved it to New York for the fall and winter season.

The premises on Barrow Street had once been a stable that housed the horses and carriage of an old patrician family and had been empty for years when Frances discovered the place. She fell in love with it. She wanted it just like it was: the high ceiling; brick walls; the creaking, wide floorboards; the two potbelly stoves; and the old forge still intact and operative. She wouldn't change a thing. She spread some fishing nets on the walls, placed a few anchors around, and plugged in some colored ship's lanterns. Then she installed barrels to sit on and bigger barrels supporting planks to eat off. She brought her Portuguese chef down from Provincetown. The food was good and I could afford it once in a while.

Frances didn't know that the winter of 1934 would be one of

the bitterest ever to hit New York. The two potbelly stoves and the forge she kept fueling with logs and coal were helpless against the glacial blasts that assaulted the stable.

I walked in for dinner one February night. There were four customers in overcoats sitting on barrels, eating. I sat down on a barrel and ordered the hot soup. When I lifted the soup spoon, it was so cold I had to lay it down quickly.

Frances, wearing a fur coat, walked over to me. "It's no use," she said.

She'd been hoping for the freezing weather to relent, but it didn't seem it ever would. She had decided to close up and go back to Provincetown. Could I use her barrels? I could have them for seventy-five dollars, which she would take out in due bills once the Vanguard opened.

Barney moved the barrels to the Vanguard in his truck. Harry placed them along the walls and on the freshly painted cement floor. I hired Johnny, the Portuguese chef from The White Whale, to take charge of the kitchen.

Everything was in place. We were ready to open.

On February 26, 1934, at nine P.M., I turned on the radio so that the first arrivals would have music to greet them. I stood myself at the door; I was the cashier and the maitre d'. All the cafeterias in the Village were empty that night. At ten o'clock, show time, Maxwell Bodenheim rose to his feet and demanded quiet. He welcomed the new Vanguard, then recited one of his poems and sat down. John Rose Gildea followed him, then Joseph Ferdinand Gould. They were all glad that the Village Vanguard had made it at last.

I stood at my station near the door till four A.M., watching everything and everybody, on the lookout for congestion or trouble, taking the pulse of the room. People were starting to leave, and I kept thinking, "I'm open, I'm really open!"

There are always the laggards at closing time, but they too finally made it up the steps. As was my habit, I took a last look around to see if any live cigarette butts were left lying around. I had my keys in my hand when two cops came walking down the steps.

"Are you the owner?" they wanted to know. I said nothing. I was new in the nightclub business, but I knew enough not to give a straight answer to a cop. They knew I was the owner and handed me the piece of paper they brought with them. It was a summons to appear in the Jefferson Market court at nine that morning to show cause why the Vanguard shouldn't be closed for presenting entertainment without a license.

It was a tense moment a few hours later when the judge asked me what I had to say for myself. I said, "Your Honor, that was no entertainment. That was poets reciting, chanting, declaiming poetry to each other."

"Dismissed," said His Honor.

That's how the Vanguard ran for a year. The cops left me alone. But I knew if I was ever to get anywhere in the nightclub business, I'd have to find another place with two johns, two exits, two hundred feet away from a church or synagogue or school, and with the rent under $100 a month. I was fed up standing all night in front of the door of the lone john in the joint shooing female customers away when there was a man inside.

And I found that place, another basement, an ex-speakeasy on Seventh Avenue South that had been "closed for alterations" for two years. I moved in overnight. Barney made five round-trips with his truck, transporting the barrels and wooden benches, second-hand tables and chairs I'd collected, the upright piano, everything except the kitchen stove. There was a six-burner Vulcan range left over by the last speakeasy over in the new place. I didn't lose one night's business.

And that's where the Village Vanguard is today.

3 : Poetry and Booze, or A Night at the Village Vanguard

In 1935 Eli Siegel was the master of ceremonies at the Village Vanguard. He ran the show and introduced the poets and the Village personalities who made their home at the Vanguard: Maxwell Bodenheim, John Rose Gildea, Joseph Ferdinand Gould, Genevieve Larssen, Harry Kemp, Jack Sellers, the National Maritime Union poet, and others, published and unpublished.

He'd bring on Abraham Lincoln Gillespie, Jr., the "Poet of Sputter," Eli called him. Eli explained that Link hailed from Philadelphia, "has been living in Paris for several years—an exile in Paris—but is back in America now and has taken up residence in Greenwich Village. Link will recite his famous Dada poem he brought back from Paris with him, 'Willow Cafeteria.' I don't want you to miss a word of it, so please be quiet," Eli warned.

Link would rise, lay down his cigarette, decline the spotlight and, in a mighty voice, start his famous poem, "Willow Cafeteria." It lasted three minutes—a clangorous babble of a busy, crazy kitchen, dishes crashing, pots and pans exploding, all mixed with stentorian cries of distress. Link had the voice for it.

He'd stop as suddenly as he began, bow, and sit down. This was a major nightly event, and never failed to bring down the house.

Eli was famous for having won the 1925 *Nation* magazine poetry prize for "Hot Afternoons Have Been in Montana." But he'd begin the nightly proceedings with his shorter poems or a poem by Vachel Lindsay, his favorite American poet. But when the requests got so hot that the audience couldn't be denied, Eli

26

would consent to recite his famous prize winner. This was a signal for the hecklers.

"When were you in Montana on a hot afternoon?" they'd cry.

Eli knew how to handle hecklers. "I wasn't in the Ford Theater when Lincoln was shot either. I know he was shot. You know he was shot. Who said you gotta be in a place to write about a place, wise guy?"

Hooting, laughter, and applause. It was all part of the fun, part of the action. You came to the Vanguard to hear the poets, watch the characters, get loaded, and heckle Eli.

In addition to poetry, there was music and the dance. Mascato, the house operatic baritone, sang, mostly "Figaro" from *The Barber of Seville*, which brought a shower of dimes, quarters, and half-dollars hurtling at his feet. I stood around with a quarter in my hand to shill for him.

Then Maggie Egri, the hat-check girl who doubled as song-stress, and Oronzo Gasparo, an artist by day and Vanguard waiter by night, were introduced by Eli. Their big number was "Rose of Washington Square." Maggie carried Oronzo piggyback off the dance floor at the end.

During the intermission a radio played dance music. Since the Vanguard didn't have a liquor license, people brought their own and ordered glasses, ice, and soda.

John Rose Gildea was welcome at every table. Joe Gould too, if he was looking for a drink. Bodenheim kept a pint bottle hidden in his back pocket. He sneaked his drinks in the men's room. Eli never took a drink, which didn't endear him to the other poets.

Eli would stand waiting for the audience to grow quiet so that the show could go on. He was not a sunny, happy, loquacious M.C. He needed quiet and, by God, he was going to get it. "I shall begin by reciting the shortest poem in the world:

"*I.*
Why?"

This set off a wave of hooting and hilarity. "Who? You?" echoed from every corner. Eli would stand firm and wait for the noise to subside. "I will now recite the second shortest poem in the world:

"*Jones Moans.*"

Laughter and applause.

These were the years of deepening depression. You could spend a night at the Vanguard for a buck. If you were broke and a member of the Greenwich Village Cafeteria Society, you were in free. A promise not to go around with a glass in your hand, mooching drinks, was the price of admission.

Eli, pale, bent, dour, with the look of a Hasid, kept the show moving. I paid him thirty a week.

Eli had to catch Gildea early if he was going to get him to recite; otherwise John was asleep in a chair. Eli liked John, as one poet to another, despite John's drinking habits.

"'The Roué Moon,' please, John," Eli'd prompt him as John labored to the floor. John not only was a poet, he looked like a poet, people said on seeing John for the first time.

"I wrote this poem when I was drunk," John would say, introducing it.

> "The roué moon wears night like a high hat—hey! hey!
> The ribald moon carries a graceful shaft,
>   malacca stick—how! how!
> The unsteady moon throws night its opera cloak
> Giggling with stars—ho, hum."

"That's poetry! That's real poetry!" Eli would say as John sat down. "Thank you, John." Eli'd then squint around the room to see who was in a condition to go on next. If no one was ready, he'd do a couplet of his own, this time in Yiddish:

> "A *fa-SHIST*
> *Passt NISHT*"

(Translation: A fascist is unbecoming, an embarrassment.)

"Joe, where are you?" Eli would then shout. "Ladies and gentlemen, the Harvard terrier and *boulevardier*, Joseph Ferdinand Gould!" How did Joe Gould deserve these mighty accolades bestowed by Eli? Joe was a Harvard graduate, class of 1912, five foot three inches tall and weighed ninety pounds. He was a man of poverty and dignity and was quick to take offense. If he felt patronized, he'd invite you outside. Thus his nickname "Harvard terrier." As for *"boulevardier,"* that's because Joe always sported a long cigarette holder.

Eli's introductions tended to be descriptive and demeaning.

It took Joe a little while to get into the amber spotlight where Eli was waiting. He had first to find a safe place for the dozen or so grammar school composition books he was always carrying around, the manuscript of his *History of the World from Oral Sources*, a work that had been in progress for twenty years when I first met Joe in the Village.

"It took four years at Harvard to make me what I am today," Joe would begin. "People sometimes ask me how I live. Air, ketchup, self-esteem, cowboy coffee, fried-egg sandwiches, cigarette butts—what else is new? What's my religion? I'm from New England. In the winter I'm a Buddhist, in the summer I'm a Nudist. And now you can make a contribution to the Joseph Ferdinand Gould fund, if you care to. You can find me at a table later."

Bodenheim, pacing and scowling in the back during Joe's performance, would stop suddenly, point his finger, and shout, "Eli Siegel! I hate you, Eli Siegel. You rat!"

Bodenheim didn't like Joe Gould's self-demeaning performance and blamed Eli. The audience hooted and applauded. Eli would then call John to the floor again to join Joe for the poem that was to follow, and also call up Professor Woodman, "who happens to be visiting us tonight." The professor, an instructor in literature at the University of Iowa and a secret poet, never failed to visit the Vanguard when in New York.

"The next poem is 'Ambition.' 'Ambition,'" Eli explained, "is a poem that has to be recited by three poets."

Gildea then assumed the role of spokesman.

"Quiet, goddamit!"

Gildea liked to do this poem because Professor Woodman, his friend, "who wrote it, is here tonight" and further because "Ambition" not only took three poets to recite, as Eli rightly said, but it was a poem that had to be assaulted, beaten, by God, to extract its full, its glorious meaning.

"So quiet, goddamit!"

Joe, John, and the visiting professor from Iowa lined themselves up, their right arms extended, poised as if about to administer a karate blow on some hidden target.

"Ambition," they'd cry, and down came their arms in anger on the unhappy word. Then together:

> *"What?*
> *Have we?*
> *To do?*

With that!
Foul bitch!
That Stinking!
Witch!"

By this time their shouts and flailing arms raised so much heat that the rest of the words got lost, and it was a good time to call another intermission to cool the place down, which Eli did.

To get the Vanguard quiet again after an intermission was no easy matter. Many times Joe Buff, the bouncer, and I would have to throw a couple of characters out of the place.

Eli liked to interject a note of seriousness, a lesson to be learned at this point:

"It often happens with a floozy
When tired and maybe boozy,
She sees her past and gets quite woozy."

What effect Eli's rhymed warning had on the customers is hard to say.

Eli would wait for Bodenheim to shape up so he could call on him to recite. But it was no use. Bodenheim, swirling crazily, eyes glazed, arms outstretched, would suddenly stop and point his finger at a frightened girl who had refused him a dance during intermission. "Rat!" he'd shout at her.

So, despairing of Bodenheim, Eli called on Baudelaire instead, and someone in the room shouted, "Is Baudelaire here tonight?"

"No, Wise guy, Baudelaire isn't here tonight, but he was a famous French poet, and I'm going to recite *one* line out of *one* of his poems, if that's all right with you," Eli said, his eyes riveted on the heckler who dared to interrupt him. "He wrote, and I quote, 'Anywhere, anywhere, out of this world.' That's a fine Village sentiment, but Baudelaire took hashish and destroyed himself. Think about it."

This serious mood upon him, Eli continued. "Take Edna St. Vincent Millay. She wrote some beautiful poetry. She wrote about burning a candle at both ends, which makes a lovely light. All very nice, very lovely, very Villagey. I don't know how you can burn a candle at both ends that makes a lovely light. I never tried it. But, to her credit, Edna St. Vincent Millay also wrote a serious poem about Sacco and Vanzetti.

"You don't know that, do you?" Eli'd say, his eyes still on the unhappy heckler.

About this time Harry Kemp, drunk—you could hear him outside calling my name—would come roistering down the steps. "Where are you, you old sonofabitch? Where's my wine? Where's the glass of wine you promised me, you old bastard?"

Harry, six feet tall, barrel-chested, hair over his eyes, would grab my shoulders and plant a kiss on my forehead. "Sit down a minute," he'd cry, pulling me toward a chair.

"That's Harry Kemp!" Eli would call out. "A fine poet and the author of 'Tramping on Life.'"

Some earnest tourist, at hearing Harry Kemp's name and anxious to be of help, would come forth, a glass of wine in his hand.

"I don't want your wine," Harry'd shout at him, then place his head on his folded arms and sob. "I don't want your goddam wine!"

Towards the end of an evening Eli liked to call on Bob Clairmont, known in Village circles as a millionaire playboy-poet. The story went that some years before, Bob, tall, handsome, muscular, when employed as a lifeguard at a private beach on Long Island one summer, had taught an aging corporate executive how to swim. The executive died and, out of simple gratitude, left Bob a million dollars in his will—or was it only four hundred grand as some Villagers claimed? It didn't matter. It didn't take Bob long, with the help of his Village cronies, to fritter away that fortune. Bob, now broke and a poet, had the privilege of a free pass to the Village Vanguard.

Bob was too shy to recite his own poetry, so Eli never pressed him. Instead, Eli recited portions of it:

> *"When I am bald and dead,*
> *With my silk hat in my hand,*
> *To the hungry worms I'll say,*
> *You still don't understand."*

Eli liked to lay these chilling lines on the crowd that had raised so much hell all night.

It all added up to a night at the Village Vanguard, a night of Greenwich Village high jinks, of poets, WPA. writers, hustlers, insomniacs, college students from the Bronx and Brooklyn, tourists, broads on the make, musicians, moochers, all of them crowding the place every night to let off steam.

I was at the Vanguard every night. I had to be, or the joint might have blown up.

But when I wasn't looking, or so it seemed to me, a lot of guys and gals who didn't belong in the place began to find their way to the Vanguard. Stags from New Jersey and the Bronx, dropouts from MacDougal Street, Irish kids from Hudson Street, all walked in carrying bottles in brown paper bags. (I still didn't have a liquor license.)

How it happened I didn't know. I didn't run any ads; I didn't have a publicity man. They didn't come to hear Eli and the poets. They came to drink beer and raise hell in the Village. And wise guys and pranksters started coming around to drive me crazy.

And on top of everything else, Eli was growing more dour and cranky than usual. Instead of sparring with the hecklers for laughs like he used to, he'd come down heavy on them, scold and snort as if he wished they were somewhere else—not at the Vanguard—and that he too, God willing, was somewhere else. It was enough. The Vanguard was due for a change, I told myself. Get rid of some of the customers, get rid of Eli, get rid of the poets and poetry and put some prose into the joint. So I did.

Eli later became the founder, leader, guru, rabbi—take your pick—of a movement he called Aesthetic Realism. Don't ask me what aesthetic realism is about. He ran it from a store on Greene Street in the Village. And he had a host of believers who followed the teachings of Aesthetic Realism. He was putting this movement together when he was the M.C. at the Vanguard. He told me this once when I ran into him on Jane Street almost forty years later. I didn't believe it.

"You need Aesthetic Realism in your life," he said, looking me in the eye. "I know the kind of man you are. It'll straighten you out. And not only you—it can straighten out the whole world. Aesthetic Realism can straighten out the whole world, if only the world will listen to me."

I see now what ailed Eli when he was the Vanguard M.C., why he was always getting so mad at the customers. He was trying to straighten them out, that's what he was doing. It's a good thing I got rid of him.

One thing I learned in almost fifty years of running a club in New York: You don't try to straighten people out in a nightclub. You leave them alone and hope they'll leave you alone.

4 : Judy and the Kids

It was 1939, and the Village Vanguard was four years old. There were nights when I'd sit in the back and talk to a pretty, shy, blonde girl, sixteen, maybe seventeen years old, who used to hang out in the place. She'd come in with a guy, or with another girl, or alone. She hung out in the Village, like a lot of kids, because she could breathe more freely, so to speak, than uptown, where she lived with her mother.

I learned that her name was Judy and that she had a job running the switchboard at Orson Welles's Mercury Theatre. She was biding her time running Orson Welles's switchboard. She said what she really wanted to do was to be on the stage at the Mercury Theatre or on any other stage—write, act, produce, do anything that involved the theater. And someday she was going to make it happen.

On the nights when she didn't show up at the Vanguard, she was with some kids in a loft uptown, at work—writing, rewriting skits and blackouts, composing and rehearsing songs and special material, and performing the stuff to each other and to any friends who happened to drop into the loft.

"What kind of skits and songs?" I asked her.

"Skits and songs of satire and social significance," she said.

I had just seen *Pins and Needles*, the International Ladies Garment Workers Union hit musical on Broadway, and I knew what she was talking about.

"Ours are a little different," she said. "What we need is an audience."

"You've got an audience—me!"

"The Village Vanguard would be a perfect place for us," she said.

I decided that I should run up to her loft and sit in on Judy and the Kids, get a look at what they were up to, which I did. I met the others: Betty, Adolph, John, and Alvin. After looking them over, I invited them down to the Village Vanguard to look me over. Except for Judy, they'd never seen the place.

I remember them walking in one night—a scared bunch. I decided to try them out, see how they felt in the room. What could I lose?

I'll always remember the night they auditioned. Seated at one table were Judy's mother, grandmother, and uncle. Her uncle had invited several of his cronies from the Cafe Royale on Second Avenue, the hangout for the Yiddish intelligentsia of the day. Judy's father, with some fellow labor union activists, was at another table.

Nearby were Adolph's father and brother; Betty's future husband, Steven; John's wife; and Alvin's wife-to-be. Fellow students of John's and Betty's from the N.Y.U. Department of Drama sat smiling and expectant.

A few outsiders dropped in, not knowing what was on the Vanguard entertainment menu that night. The poets, having been warned, stayed away, except for Bodenheim, who was seated at a table in the back, obviously asleep.

With John at the piano, the Kids went into their opening number, in which they explained how happy they were to be at the Village Vanguard to sing about New York. The opening number sounded as if it had been written the night before. It had, Judy told me later. They loved New York, but they had some beefs about New York that they were now going to sing about. They hoped we'd like them.

I listened to the show and to the reaction of the audience. I expected Judy's mother, father, and uncle to like it, but I found myself liking it, too.

When the show was over, Bodenheim rose from his chair, pointed a finger at the Kids, shouted, "Bah! Amateurs! Rats! You stink!" and stormed out of the door.

It scared the hell out of them.

But I hired them on the spot.

Now that they had an audience, they needed a name for the act. I thought "Judy and the Kids" was a great name. Judy thought different. Their act was a cooperative venture, Judy explained, and she didn't want her name up there. It took them a month to come up with a name. The Revuers they finally decided to call themselves, which was all right with me. So this was how the sign read outside the door: THE REVUERS. TWO SHOWS A NIGHT. APPEARING EVERY NIGHT. MINIMUM CHARGE $1.00.

The Kids worked every night, seven nights a week. They did the same show every night for a week, and afternoons they worked on next week's show. They thought they needed a new show every week. So on Mondays at noon, we'd gather in the diner on Sixth Avenue and Eighth Street and, over hamburgers and ketchup, the writing of next week's show would begin. Betty, a yellow pad before her, a pencil in her hand, was the script girl. Everybody brought ideas. I was there because I was the only one with a key to the Vanguard, where we headed after some coffee.

I remember the first whiff of stale air every time I unlocked the Vanguard door. We kept our coats on. I put a match to the antiquated gas heaters to take the early chill off the place. Then we'd pull some chairs off the tables and sit down. I'd hang around, fascinated, listening to songs and lyrics, skits and blackouts emerge and take shape. And then I'd watch the rehearsals and the rewriting that followed.

Not until people began calling for old numbers did it occur to them that they didn't have to write a new show every week, that they could put their best old numbers into one show, run it for a month, and catch up on some sleep.

One night, when they had been at the Vanguard for six weeks, Betty and Adolph, on their way to work, couldn't get into the place. The stairs were mobbed with people trying to get in.

"I can't get in. What's going on?" Betty asked. She was calling from a pay phone across the street. "And they're out into the street!" she said incredulously.

"Come to the back door. I'll let you in. It's that write-up Dick Manson did in the *Post* yesterday."

Dick Manson, the drama critic of the New York *Post*, had been hearing through the grapevine about five "upstart kids" doing some wild material in a basement in the Village, and he decided to find them and catch their act.

That did it. Here's what the critic wrote in the *Post* the next day:

They knocked me out! The freshest, funniest, brightest, most original material I have ever seen in a nightclub.

How can I ever give you some idea of the kind of show it is? One skit spoofs the press. Ouch! There's been a murder in the Bronx. The *Graphic* runs a picture of the victim lying in his blood, on the front page. The *Sun*, a simpering interview with the widow and neighbors on the block. The *Times* has it on page 28, a short paragraph, "Another Murder in the Bronx." I'm not telling you how the *Post* handled this dastardly crime. The same murder, a different story. "So what paper d'you read?" Judy cries, wrapping it up.

It was funny.

"Beefs" about New York these kids call their show.

Up steps Betty to announce the next "beef"—the 6th Avenue L is being dismantled and the scrap sold to Japan. She's against it and hopes New York is against it.

The skit that followed showed the kids huddled in a trench in No Man's Land in California, defending their native land against the Japanese invader, as bombs labeled "Made in N.Y." are raining down on them.

The skit has some production problems, I'll admit, but the point is clear and I found it vastly amusing.

Then Judy—a pretty kid—looks like she's 16, comes on and sings a song about the World's Fair, "The World's Fair in Unfair," she laments. Dressed in a flowing white robe and the spiked crown of the Statue of Liberty she complains that tourists are fickle and have been neglecting her since the World's Fair opened in Flushing in 1936. It's now 1939 and time they were back. "I've been carrying a torch for fifty years. And I'll be here long after Flushing is a dump again."

It was fun. We're all tired of the World's Fair, and I loved it.

It's now Adolph's turn, and with John Frank at the piano, Adolph steps forward and sings out Grieg's "Flight of the Bumblebee" in one minute flat—which brings the house down.

A great bunch of kids. Their names: "The Revuers" they call themselves, are: Judy Holliday, Betty Comden, Adolph Green, John Frank and Alvin Hammer. And they're wonderful!

So run, don't walk, if you want a night you'll always remember.

After a write-up like that, no wonder all of New York was trying to get into the Vanguard.

The crowds didn't affect The Kids though. It was good to have an audience, great to see the place jammed every night, but what really set them buzzing with excitement was when it was whispered that George Abbott, Fred Astaire, Noël Coward, or Bea Lillie was in the audience. The Kids didn't care about the crowds; they wanted to be seen by the right people, who might, if they liked them, open doors to the magic world of the theater to them. For that's where they were headed.

One night after their first show, Judy came over to me and said she wanted to talk to me about something important. "A man by the name of Mr. Roy," she began, "the managing director he told me he was of The Rainbow Room, a nightclub on top of Rockefeller Plaza. . ."

"Yes, I know," I said, fearing what was coming.

"He wants us. He wants to put us in The Rainbow Room. He'll pay us two hundred fifty a week, and he paints a pretty picture: 'From a basement in Greenwich Village to the sixty-fifth floor of Rockefeller Plaza.' What shall we do?"

"Take it," I said.

What was I supposed to do? Try to stop them? The Vanguard was the first rung on the ladder; maybe The Rainbow Room was their next step up. I knew what the Kids were thinking about. So when Judy let me have it, I said, "OK, take it and good luck."

I can't keep an act like that forever, I reasoned.

They made me a present of a silver cigarette case engraved "To Max from the Kids" and left a hole in the Village Vanguard.

I didn't get dressed and go uptown to their opening in The Rainbow Room.

I thought I'd never see those kids again. They'd never come back to the Vanguard after The Rainbow Room—and for three years I didn't know what happened to them.

I opened The Blue Angel on East Fifty-fifth Street in 1943. One day I got this letter from an agent:

Could you use The Revuers at The Blue Angel for two weeks? You remember the act. But the money this time has got to be different from the kind of money you paid the five

of them at the Vanguard in 1940—one hundred twenty-five
a week.

It took me a week to sell my partner Jacobi on the idea.

A month later The Revuers came to New York and opened at
The Blue Angel. They were as great at The Blue Angel as they
were at the Vanguard. Stayed not two weeks but six, and left.

After they left New York, I heard their agent sent them all
over the map, opening and closing them in every "dine and
dance" palace in every honky-tonk town from Chicago to Los
Angeles.

Somebody saw them at the Trocadero in Hollywood.

Then I heard something happened to the Kids' act, something
I thought could never happen. An actor who regularly traveled
the Hollywood–New York circuit ran into them in Hollywood and
brought the news with him to New York. The kids were feeling
they had no future as an act. They'd been together five years.
Nothing was happening. So they decided one day to break it up,
separate, and each go off by himself to wherever it may lead in
show business.

Judy stayed in Hollywood. Betty and Adolph came to New
York. What happened to John and Alvin nobody seemed to
know.

What was going to happen to those kids now, I asked when I
heard what they did to themselves. I didn't hear about them
again for a year. One Sunday in *The New York Times* I read that
the musical comedy *On the Town*, written by Betty Comden and
Adolph Green with music by Leonard Bernstein, was opening on
Broadway. I got myself a couple of tickets. The next morning the
critics called it a hit.

Judy came to New York the next year and opened in a play of
her own, *Kiss Them for Me*, in which she played a supporting
role, "the part of a dumb little tart," one critic called it. She stole
the show and won the Clarence Derwent prize of five hundred
dollars for that year.

"That five hundred is going to come in handy," Judy's mother,
Helen, whispered to me when I ran into her in the lobby of the
theatre that afternoon.

Maybe those kids knew what they were doing after all,
breaking up the act, I remember saying to my wife.

Kiss Them for Me didn't last long on Broadway. Two years

later, in 1946, Judy opened in *Born Yesterday* this time in a starring role, playing the part of Billie Dawn, another "dumb broad." It looked like Judy's specialty was playing "dumb broads." It ran two years. Later she took it to Hollywood and made a movie for which she won an Academy Award.

I followed Judy's name in the papers. She married, divorced, became the mother of a son, was seen with Syd Chaplin, the son of Charlie Chaplin—"a torrid affair," one columnist called it. Judy was a star and made good copy.

One day I received two tickets in the mail from Judy. They were for the opening of *Bells Are Ringing* at the Shubert Theater, a new musical comedy, written for her by Betty Comden and Adolph Green, with music by Jule Styne.

I went backstage after the show, embraced Judy, and ran into Betty and Adolph.

"We're together again," I remember Judy saying to me. "Us kids are together again."

The show ran two and a half years at the Shubert, and then toured with Judy.

After it closed Judy returned to Hollywood to star in the film version with Dean Martin. She was forever returning to Hollywood, then doubling back to New York. "I can't stand Hollywood," she once told me.

When she rented a large apartment in The Dakota on Central Park West, I knew she was at last going to make New York her home. I learned only later how gravely ill she was.

One night in the mid-sixties, who should come walking down the steps of the Vanguard by herself but Judy, dressed in mink. It was 2 A.M. and Gerry Mulligan and his jazz quartet were about to go on for the last set of the night. Gerry was a regular at the Vanguard during this time, played there three or four times a year, once with a band of seventeen men.

So here was Judy after all these years, a star, famous, a celebrity, come down to see the old place again (more likely to hear Gerry, with whom her name was being coupled in the gossip columns lately—"another torrid affair"). All that hadn't changed her. She was as shy, as beautiful, as glad to be here as she was when she worked at the Vanguard with the other kids. We sat down on a bench in the back to listen to the music. Then one of my multifarious duties called me—it never failed. I left my seat for a moment, and when I got back, she was gone. Where'd she go? She was in the kitchen playing Scrabble with the kitchen man whom she hadn't seen for more than twenty years.

We closed up and took a cab up to Reuben's on Fifty-eighth Street for a late sandwich like we used to. I reminded Judy of another cab ride up to Reuben's—how she had the cabbie stop in front of the place, told us to wait, she'd be right back, because she had an important errand to perform inside. I found out later what her errand was. She wanted to make sure there was a table available in the place. She put the headwaiter on the spot so that there'd be no hassle, no embarrassment, no turndown at the door when we walked in with Eddie Heywood, a jazz musician in our party, a black man who was playing at the Vanguard. She was surprised I remembered it.

I had always wanted to ask Judy what happened to her and the Kids at The Rainbow Room.

"We bombed. That's what happened," she said. "Opening night the M.C., dressed in tails, introduced us after the ballroom dance team. 'The Revuers,' he cried, 'a quintet from Greenwich Village,' he called us a quintet, 'doing original songs and skits,' which he hoped they'd all like. So out we walked, five ill-assorted kids, smiling and scared to death.

"I couldn't see the audience. I could only hear them . . . eating. We did one of our less brilliant performances, to put it mildly. We weren't a smooth, fast-moving act that could wow an audience," she continued. "We weren't an act. We were a Vanguard act. We made mistakes. The Vanguard forgave us our mistakes. Even when we were bad, we were good." She smiled at the thought.

"Thank God when the four weeks were over. So there we were, without jobs. 'Let's go home and wait,' I said. But Alvin and John had wives to support. So we hired an agent. For years we trudged up and down the land in buses and trains doing our act. No place ever seemed to want to have us back.

"I thought we'd about reached the end of the road. One day, I think we had just closed a particularly dismal weekend in Cleveland, we received a wire from our agent. The Fox studio was casting a picture titled *Greenwich Village*. They wanted us. They wanted our act for a part in the film, a small part, not much money, but a great opportunity. You know the pitch. Who knew what it might lead to?

"This was it! Hollywood! At last! What we've been waiting for. A picture called *Greenwich Village*. It sounded like perfect casting.

"So there we were in Hollywood," Judy continued. "Living in a crummy four-room apartment on Sunset Boulevard, cooking our meals and washing our laundry, waiting to hear our fate.

"Our agent brought us the news. The studio had finally finished cutting the picture. Except for a single line—'Here's your hat,' delivered by Betty to Don Ameche—all the scenes we appeared in ended up on the cutting room floor. 'Nice kids, talented, original, promising kids, but not right for *Greenwich Village*,' was the studio's verdict.

"It was a disaster. The studio was interested only in me. They wanted to sign me to a seven-year contract. They didn't want the other kids. Our agent had the contract in his pocket. I'd have to lose some weight, that's all.

"The scene in that apartment was like a grade-B movie. I refused to sign the contract and walk out on the Kids and break up the act. Betty and Adolph said, 'Sign it! Don't worry about the act.' The agent kept crying, 'It's your big chance!' John and Alvin stood by, silent and miserable."

"I always wanted to write, but I ended up an actress, not the best maybe but an actress. Betty and Adolph wanted to act, so they became wonderful writers—*Billion Dollar Baby, Wonderful Town, Singing in the Rain, Peter Pan*, great musicals they kept pounding out. They wrote *Bells Are Ringing* for me. 'I can't sing,' I said to them. 'Yes, you can,' they said. So I did, first time I ever was in a musical show on Broadway. Betty and Adolph said I could do it."

"What happened to John and Alvin?" I asked her.

Judy looked grave a moment, then said, "John and Alvin were wonderful and talented. John is a fine musician and composer. We all wrote music and lyrics at the Vanguard. John could really play the piano. And Alvin, a great comedian. I remember the first time I saw Alvin teamed up with Phil Leeds, two funny guys.

"We found each other—us kids—when we were all looking to get a wedge into the theater. You gave us a job. We needed each other then. Then we didn't need each other," she said sadly.

"Let's keep in touch," we promised each other. And for years we did. We kept in touch. Then with the passing years we lost touch."

One night about a year before Judy died in 1965, my wife, Lorraine, and I had dinner with her and her son in her apartment. She was still well enough to cook it herself. After dinner, she brought out a bottle of liqueur.

"Do you remember this?" she asked me. "You used to get us a half-pint bottle. We'd keep it in our dressing room, which was the hallway leading to the ladies' room. I'd take a quick swig to steady my nerves before going on every night.

"Nightclubs used to scare me. They still do. Playing a role on the stage is a cinch compared to playing in a nightclub. You're protected on the stage. You're not out there playing yourself, where they can get at you. I don't see how I stood it all these years."

5 : Josh, Leadbelly, Woody Guthrie, and the Blues

It was 1941, and I was desperately looking for an act to take the place of Judy and the Kids. "Where am I ever going to find another one like that again?" I asked Nick Ray. "Where do I look first?"

Nick was a friend of Judy's and had seen Judy and the Kids' show a dozen times at the Vanguard. He couldn't understand it, he told me, when he heard they were leaving; why would they want to leave a place like the Vanguard for a place like The Rainbow Room?

"They've got a long way to go," he said, "and if they'd have asked me I'd've told 'em, 'stay where you are and learn your business.'"

Nick was living in the Village, at the Almanac House on Sixth Avenue, "waiting for something to happen." It happened—but that was years later, when he ended up in Hollywood directing pictures. He directed a lot of pictures in Hollywood, some good, some bad. His best was *Rebel Without a Cause*, starring Jimmy Dean and Natalie Wood. I have yet to see it.

Nick told me about a singer he'd heard, one Huddie Ledbetter, "Leadbelly," he called him, who had just arrived in New York from Washington, D.C., where he cut a lot of records for the Library of Congress.

"Leadbelly's songs is history," Nick emphasized, and the Library of Congress wants them for its archives in order to preserve them for posterity.

He gave me a quick rundown of the Leadbelly story: that

43

Leadbelly years before had been serving a life sentence for murder in a Texas state penitentiary. The governor of the state used to pay the penitentiary periodic visits of inspection, on which occasions the warden would organize entertainment by the prisoners for the governor's party. Leadbelly was the star entertainer.

Every time the governor came around, he'd ask for Leadbelly. He remembered him from the last time and wanted to hear him again. The governor, as events turned out, lost his bid for reelection. And on his last night as governor, who does he remember but Leadbelly, rotting away in prison. As his last official act, he decides to free him.

"The governor must've felt," Nick added, "that Leadbelly was probably an innocent man anyway, because it was easy for a black man to get himself into trouble in Texas in those years.

"And Leadbelly's here in New York now, looking for a job, a place to sing those same songs that sung him out of prison, songs he's sung in boom town honky-tonks from Texas City to Butte, Montana, on the Copper Hill. He wants to sing 'em in New York.

"And there's another black folk singer in New York too, looking for a job—Josh White. Josh is different. He plays a blues guitar, the greatest blues guitar in the land. Together they'd make a great folk singing team. I'll put them together for you, build their act, and you'll have the greatest folk singing act in the country—if you're still looking for an act."

So one afternoon we met in front of the Vanguard—Nick, Josh, Leadbelly, and me. I unlocked the front door, locked it from the inside, and we walked down the cement steps. I turned on the work-lamp, wiped a table clean, and put a bottle of rye on the table.

I hung around, watching and listening, saying nothing. Not until they finished the bottle did they say anything to me. So I put another bottle on the table.

This went on for a week. And one day, twenty bottles later, Nick said he thought they were ready and when did I want them to open?

Opening night was one of those nights. There was in the place a feeling that something important was going to happen. I never saw so many guitars in the place: Pete Seeger, Burl Ives, Richard Dyer-Bennet, Millard Lampel, The Almanac Singers, five strong, and Woody Guthrie—all present, with guitars slung over their shoulders.

Josh—smooth, handsome, and bare-throated; and Leadbelly, in high "yaller" shoes, his powerful frame immaculately attired in a powder blue suit. Josh did "Great God A'Mighty Folks a'Feelin' Bad." Leadbelly did "Boll Weevil," "Bottle Up & Go," and "Take This Hammer." They did "Grey Goose" together, and the crowd sang along with them. They finished carving each other out on their guitars.

Nick came over and said to me, "Woody thinks we need a mike for Leadbelly. I don't think so. Huddie's got enough power in his own voice to move a mountain." I was glad Nick felt that way, because the Vanguard owned one mike and Josh was using it.

Nobody moved when intermission came. They were waiting for the second show. I sat down next to Woody Guthrie. "What do you think?" I asked him.

"You know what I think?" he began. "You know what I think of Josh and Huddie?"

I found out what he thought two days later when I received this letter from him:

> Almanac Singers
> 130 West 10th St.,
> New York City.

Village Vanguard,
Dear Max & Everybody:

The opening at your place of your new show featuring Josh White and Leadbelly has got all that it takes to make real night club history in New York, and to give the Negro people a real honest chance to bring their music and singing before the general public in such a way that will not only please your own customers, but will have a big influence on lots of other night club owners, showmen, radio men, etc., and the likes; and open up a whole new field for entertainers of all colors, namely just plain, common, everyday American Music.

If I had lots of money I'd be pretty religious about coming

down and listening to Josh and Huddie, but I'll still drop in as often as the law and my pocketbook allows. And I did promise you that I'd jot down some of the ideas that I had about the show.

You can show this letter to Nick Ray if you want to, because, although he's staying here at the Almanac house for a few days right now, till he can find him another place, I suppose this letter will be in the mail before he gets a chance to look it over.

Josh and Huddie come from my kind of people, and they're carrying on a great tradition in the line of Blind Lemon Jefferson, one of the really great blues singers and guitar players. To really know Josh and Leadbelly, you've first got to know and understand the blues and what the blues mean to different people from different places. It's a pretty good idea, too, to know something about their days spent leading Blind Lemon around over the country, the boom town honky tonks down south, through the midwest and the west, from Texas City on the gulf, to Butte Montana on the Copper Hill . . . but that would take a regular magazine article. This is just a friendly letter.

Josh is an intelligent young guy, fast thinker, easy talker— friendly, and has made his living most of his life by being just that way. He's mainly interested in showing the world what all can be done on a 6 string guitar, and by singing. He represents this same thought in the minds of millions of city people. Only Josh just happens to know the guitar and the blues 'from way back'—and this gives him the real feeling of what the blues is all about . . . the voice of the Negro people singing a worried song for all people. Josh remembers that Joe Louis is the best boxer the world ever had, and Josh wants to be the Joe Louis of the blues guitar. After lots of years of hard playing and singing Josh has got to be just that.

Leadbelly is a different character. The guitar to Leadbelly is just another way to get people to set still and listen to what he's got to say to them. He's dead serious. He's a great speaker in his own right. He tells you of life as it's hit him, and tells you how to take it easier, and miss the hard spots that he's been through, and how to have as much fun as he's had. I've thought lots of times that if I live just half the life that Leadbelly has lived, and live it as honest as he's lived it, I'll be pretty well satisfied. His big he man voice. His hard hitting talks before his songs. His theory about the blues is as short and true as theory can be. I've heard him say the same words over and over several hundred times, both at his home, and on his public appearances, and the words tell me something new every time—I think new things.

This is the same thing that showed up so plain in Blind Lemon's work, that straight out honesty, without any of the fancy trimmings, that made you actually believe the blues, the reason for the blues, the waste, and the mishandling of things that causes the blues. Huddie says, My people has got the blues about everything, about clothes, about money, about place to stay, and places that aint worth the rent you got to pay—use to be lots of people had the blues; nowdays everybody's got the blues; but the white folks blues quits where the Negro blues starts in——. I've never heard the Negro situation said any clearer or easier than that, and there are lots of progressive books and papers going around.

Then, what you have is two separate characters, and their separate talents must be built up in the peoples mind in exactly the same way that you'd say, Here's the boy from the Ukraine that destroyed a Hitler tank all by himself, and was honored with the order of Lenin. Or, here's the boy from Tennessee that sunk a German U-Boat singlehanded. The thing here is exactly what the Red Army bases most of it's morale upon, that is it's propoganda, the personal, individual accomplishments of it's soldiers in a human, warm, and friendly way, that Hitler can't afford to entertain; because he dont believe in individual thinking and doing— but that your thoughts are supposed to come from 'higher up'—and your own personal work dont amount to much. This is the secret of a constantly increasing morale in the anti-Hitler forces, and a constantly failing morale in the Axis armies—because there isn't this personal, friendly, simple human element.

So what you've got in your show is almost the equal of two of the best acts in the country, namely, Josh White on the guitar, singing the big city blues, and Huddie Leadbelly, representing the rural, country boy singing in the hot spots of the mushroom boom towns that bloom and fade, without anybody quite knowing how, why, or where to from here. It is an entire way of life with both of them and their individual feelings about their individual work can't be anything but slowed down to work both of them together too much on a show. It cramps Josh's style, and cramps Leadbelly's. Both of them personally have told me that they had slightly different ways of doing their best, and that working together as a team didn't allow their best to come through; and to present Josh and Huddie at any level but their best is wrong—because they're the kind of guys that shoot their best every time, and that's what people like to follow them around for—to enjoy the richness of their personal experiences, and to actually be entertained and educated at the same time—because being around either one of these guys for very long will surely teach you something, even if you're pretty hard headed.

They can play hot guitars together. I'm not against that. There'd ought to be a hot guitar piece or two on each show; but the hot guitar should come as a result of their different backgrounds, an actual, more outright conflict than was on either the rehearsal or the first night's show. The Carving, outdoing each other, ought to be pointed up more . . . with each standing on his own ground and proud to out-carve anybody that comes along—Leadbelly falling back on his great love for simplicity, roughness, honesty, strength, and volume, and Josh playing on the more refined, citified, educated, a little more complicated, but still mean and honest, system. It would not only add to Leadbelly's strength and power, but to Josh's tricky, smooth, talent. These are the best qualities of each one, and an outright contest, spoken, side cracked, played, even sung back and forth between them would be the talk of everybody that heard the two work.

People would learn to expect something of the same show every night at the Vanguard, but would know that there would be plenty of 'new little things' added to make their night ten times more enjoyable. They would soon be saying, Let's go down to the Vanguard and watch Leadbelly and Josh carve each other out.

There's a big pride in a feller's heart for the place that he comes from, or for the places he's been, things he's been through, and seen—and this is a dozen times moreso about the things you learned to do, no matter if you learned how to crank up a tractor and plow the straightest row, or take up the guitar and whang off the meanest blues. And if you got a job in a show that didn't allow you to 'take all comers'—(like the carnival wrestlers), you'd feel like you wasn't shooting your best shot or playing your best card. I've felt this way lots of times when cast with other people, not because of any small respect for the other people, but just sort of a matter of personal pride. You're proudest of the things you learnt how to do. You want to do them your very best. Either your best, or not at all.

You've really got a good show at the Vanguard now. Josh and Leadbelly have got thousands of friends that follow them around. The testimonial down at Cafe Society, where a couple or three hundred good cash customers were turned away because the place was overcrowded, is a good proof of that. Worked just right, there's no end to the amount of good publicity that you can get on Josh and Huddie. It is a whole peoples affair, and stories and articles can be slanted from all sorts of angles—all very progressive, all political at heart.

I'm not writing this letter to sell you a bill of goods, because I know you've already bought the goods and are just figuring how it's best to make it up into something better. I'm just writing because I'm talking about real American Singing and Music, and that's something that I've always liked better than I ever liked myself.

I thought of several possibilities. One, about Leadbelly's voice. Maybe he could work better a little more out in the middle of the floor. Either this, or try a lapel microphone, to try to get his voice a little more above his guitar. Leadbelly has mostly worked right in the big middle of crowds of people, and this seems to give him the added lick to turn out better stuff. Another thing, the crowd had ought to sing some song with him every show. Possibly the crowd should request some song, like Gray Goose, Boll Weevil, or some such number that's easy to catch onto. It would be something that very few night spots have succeeded in doing, and would make people let their hair down and limber up their reputations, and purse strings a little more. Especially their purse strings.

Josh's voice on the mike is okay. Guitar a little too loud when he really cuts loose, especially when Leadbelly is singing without electricity out in front of Josh, and down below him. This is a bad seating arrangement. They'd ought to be side by side when they work together, so neither one would have to stretch his neck a foot and a half forwards or backwards to get a glimpse at what the other guy was doing. This little glance is a big thing to all musicians, as it gives them advance ideas of what the other guy is going to do . . . . and it's impossible with Josh setting way in the back of Huddie, and Huddie so far below Josh.

Josh's 'Great God A Mighty Folks A Feelin' Bad' is a good one. I'm not any too easy in my seat about the 'Jack Rabbit that had the Habit'. His songs are pitched too mush in the same movement and tempo to suit me, all too slow beat, and smooth and sweet. This is just a little thing, but worth thinking about . . . it dont quite give you a chance to see Josh cut his okra in other rythms and styles. His talking voice when he introduces his own numbers is good enough, plain talk, ordinary, and he says a lot in a few words.

Leadbelly is a regular philosopher of chain gangs, prisons, wardens, and hard times in the country, the country where there's more of it under corn than under concrete. He's a walking talking reporter on good times and bad times, wine, women, work, and music. His advice to wondering married couples is worth the price of admission. His outspoken truth of the goodness and shortcomings of most of us, is plainer than I can tell it. He's older than most of us. Experience is on his side. And he doesn't think to pull words. He's polite. He's cultured. But it's in a rough, hard working way, and must be looked at in the same way. He's a working man, singing for working people, and has always been a gang leader in all of the work that he's had to do. And all of this is in his singing and talking. It's wrong to stage him from any other angle.

(Wait a minute till I boil me up a pot of coffee . . .) (Okay, got 'er).

Now, as far as politics goes, I aint just certain—certainly there hadn't ought to be anything that would encourage strikes in National Defense Industries, nor to run the morale of the US Army uniform down; however, Josh could sing songs of how proud he is to be working in Industry to Beat Hitler, how great it is to wear the Uniform of the good old Red White and Blue . . . and in mentioning the Army, or the war, the feeling should be this: Just about the best thing a man can wear is an Army Uniform—call for Negro Rights, equal chance, equal pay, equal treatment, but dont run down any branch of the armed service—, because a Uniform and a gun to beat Hitler with is a wonderful thing. A song by Josh about looking for a job in production for Uncle Sam's Defense would be a good thing, and even mentioning sending lots of help to everybody, everywhere, of every color, that's fighting to bring old Hitler down . . . this could be worked on.

Leadbelly is good on 'Bourgeouise Blues', 'Bottle Up & Go', and the two are best together on 'Dont Lie Buddy' . . . . possibly with some little changes in the verses by Josh.

Leadbelly's little cracks coming in while Josh is singing about work, women, etc., is fine and dandy.

Blind Lemon Jefferson is the great tradition about the whole thing, and there are lots of very good tales and antecdotes in his life that could be told by the MC to point the whole show up, give it a little more historical value, and prove the origin of this style of music by the Negroes and the spread and influence even amongst white hill country people, and even lumberjacks, gold chasers, cowboys, oil boomers, etc., somewhere in the show—because Victor's two biggest sellers, namely Jimmy Rogers, the Blue Yodeler, and the Carter Family, blues, ballad, and religious singers, have constantly used the two and three line repeat, with a last line the same. The westerners are singing almost a pure Negro style, while at work or celebrating, and lots of them haven't stopped to think yet that the whole thing traces back to the slaves, the sharecroppers, the big town workers, the chain gangs, and spiritual songs of the Negro People. This is the influence of Negro singing on everybody else in America, and it should be mentioned, and proven, somewhere on the bill, just as an interesting twist.

The MC'd ought to be very, very close friends with Josh & Leadbelly, and talk about them with a running start. I felt that the girl, while being a fine entertainer on her own part, was feeling for words while talking about the pair. If I'm mistaken here, allright. The whole note of the program is an easy, short, and simple thing—but whether it can be best told in jiving slang is doubtful to me. I think that here, as far as the MC goes, wit and humor should be the main stem, but serious, clear and some interesting historic points should be made—because PM once gave us a full 11 page of pictures about Huddie and Josh just simply because we tracked from Blind Lemon, to Huddie and Josh, and to Beating Hitler in one sentence . . . . . . publicity people, photographers and the likes, may be itching to push this stuff to the front, but waiting for some timely slant that will explain the expenditure of film, bulbs, and ink to the big boss that owns the paper. I find this the case in lots of reporters, and reviewers. That's the main secret of getting publicity—to make it rather a peoples history, instead of a drink of champagne that bubbles a little bit, and then is gone.

One more thing. I would like to get my little brother to come out here from Oklahoma and take out his saw and hammer, and just pretty near any old paint brush, scissors, etc., and sort of nail you up a display case on the front of your bldg there that would be worth the space it's taking up, look better, say more, be easier to see, and also be water and weatherproof—as well as get more moneyed customers to walk that staircase that leads to your cash register. The pictures you got out there are okay—but who in the hell designed that display case? It reminds me of a liquor joint that I went through somewhere in the deep interior of old Mexico, where a Mexican boy said, Oh, so you're on your way to DelRey . . . Yes, it's five kilos over the mountain . . . I was over there once about a year ago . . . . they got an electric light over there that burns all night . . . !

I'm drinking another cup of homemade coffee, grounds and all, to the success of your new show . . . . just like Barnum said to Bailey.

What's that friend of your's name that works for the Bonneville Power Administration out there in Portland, Oregon? He told me to tell you howdy for him, when I was hitch hiking it from coast to coast last spring. I said I would. But I never did. He also said for you to give me a job, but I never got around to that, either.

Take it easy, but take it.   True as the Average,

Woody Guthrie
11-27-'41

I could never pin Woody down. Every time I had an opening for him, he'd be off somewhere with his guitar, thumbing his way across the land, out into the country "where there was more of it under corn than under concrete"—

6 : Ten Years at the Vanguard, and How I Made It to Carnegie Hall

Richard Dyer-Bennet was born in England, raised in California, and came to New York in 1941 to break into the concert field. He was a tenor, lean, of middle height, beak-nosed, with corn-colored hair reaching down to his ears. He sang sixteenth-, seventeenth-, and eighteenth-century Scotch, Irish, and English ballads, accompanying himself on a lute. I gave him a job at the Vanguard in 1942.

About a year ago Dick and I were in a MacDougal Street restaurant, sitting over a bottle of wine, talking of the good old days at the Vanguard.

"Three years I was at it," said Dick ruefully, filling his glass. "Three years, every night, three shows a night, without a night off, until one fateful night I was rushed, exhausted and hemor-rhaging, to Bellevue Hospital. My wife, Melvene, said, 'Take a month off.' But my daughter, Bonnie, was just born. We had to eat and pay the rent."

"What was I paying you?"

"Eighty-five bucks a week. That was a raise from the fifty Herb Jacobi paid me at the Ruban Bleu. I worked there a few weeks when I got to New York. Eighty-five bucks felt like a lot of money. You upped me to a hundred fifty a year later. By the time I left, you were paying me three hundred fifty a week. I never asked you for a raise."

"It was more money than I was taking out of the joint," I said.

"I didn't come to America from London where I was born, to California where I grew up, then all the way back to New York again to sing at the Vanguard for money," he said emptying his glass. "I came to New York to break into the concert field. The Vanguard was the place I could do it best, Burl Ives told me when I got here. Develop my repertory, make mistakes, try, sing songs I wanted to. You never once told me what songs to sing."

"What the hell do I know about seventeenth-century English ballads? I never heard one until I heard you. I liked the bloody ones best, songs of mutinies and the hangings on the high seas."

"You liked 'Barbara Allen,'" protested Dick.

"It wasn't bad."

"The gentlest love song ever written," he said.

"I could sing the bloodiest or the gentlest songs at the Vanguard. You let me alone. That's what was so good about the place.

"Remember one New Year's Eve?" he continued. "The place rocking with people and their goofy hats. Eddie Heywood, the pianist, introduced me. I walked on the floor. I never used a mike. I stood there waiting for quiet, one minute, two minutes, three minutes. So, I turned around and walked off. If they didn't want to hear me, the hell with 'em. You didn't say one word to me. Another thing I liked about the Vanguard.

"At the second show you stood right next to me on the floor, looking mean. You emitted a 'shhh' that shook the house. All service stopped, the waiters stood at attention. People stopped talking, glared down people who didn't, and before I knew it a dead silence spread over the place. I opened with the quietest song, Ben Jonson's 'Where the White Lily Grows,' at midnight on a New Year's Eve!

"Burl and I were together every day, moving around New York swapping songs. I was at the Ruban Bleu; he was at the Vanguard.

"Gilbert Seldes was running an experimental TV station in the Grand Central Building for CBS that year. He heard Burl, then heard me, and engaged us both for three programs, me singing English and Scottish ballads, and Burl singing the American descendants of these ballads. A nice musical idea. I did the 'Golden Vanitee'; Burl, the 'Turkish Reverie.' We did the English and American versions of 'Barbara Allen' and 'Lord Randall,' then 'Go Tell Aunt Rodie,' together. I loved that program."

"Yeah, I remember the night Burl came over to see me," I said. He was drafted, and leaving at the end of the week. 'I got just the man to take my place,' he said. Burl's word was good enough for me. I didn't even ask you to audition, did I?"

"No, but you heard me. I came down one night, and Burl called me up to the floor. You heard me all right, before you hired me. You knew what you were doing, you bum.

"A lot of acts kept coming and going while I was at the Vanguard: Leadbelly; 'Professor' Corey, the comedian; Pearl Bailey."

"I sent 'em—some of them—up to The Blue Angel, which I opened in '43 with Herbert, your old boss at the Ruban Bleu."

"Me you kept on."

"I'll tell you why. 'Is that skinny, blond, beak-nosed English-man with the lute still singing at your place?' people would call up and ask. You were developing a following, man. That's why I kept you on, if you have to know the truth."

"Remember the night Carol Channing opened?" asked Dick. "Fresh out of Bennington College. Eddie Heywood who accom-panied her came over to me, 'What the hell did Max hire her for? She can't sing.'

"'She's a comedienne, she doesn't have to sing,' I told Eddie.

"People'd wait for the intermission to show me old songs," mused Dick, "songs their grandmothers taught them, offered to sing them for me. We'd go in the kitchen—I first heard the Irish potato famine song, 'Down Where the Praties Grow' right in your kitchen. I wrote down the music, wrote a lute arrangement, and it's been in my concert repertoire ever since. I spent more time in the Vanguard kitchen than in my kitchen at home."

"By the way, what was the name of that corporate executive from Chicago, who'd come to the Vanguard and sit at your feet every time he came to New York on business?" I asked Dick.

"Paepke—Walter Paepke, the boss of the Container Corpora-tion of America, a grand man. He was the one who offered my wife and myself some help in setting up our experimental School of Minstrelsy in Aspen, Colorado. But that came three years after Carnegie Hall.

"And you know, Max, it wasn't Sol Hurok who first put me in Carnegie Hall. It was Ted Zittel!"

"Ted who?"

"Ted! Mike Quill's publicity man—Mike Quill, of the Trans-port Worker's Union. You don't remember Ted? He and Mike'd come down every Friday night to hear me. I'd put in a couple of extra Irish ballads Friday night for Mike.

"First, Ted asked me to sing to the T.W.U. in Madison Square Garden. Then, in the spring of '44, he presented me in three recitals at Town Hall. Finally, one Friday night, Ted said to me, 'You belong in Carnegie Hall. What d'you say? You don't even have to take a night off here.'

"That's how it happened. That's how I first made it to Carnegie Hall. No, it wasn't Sol Hurok."

Dick filled his glass again, took a long breath and continued.

"But Sol Hurok was there in that august hall that November night. He heard me. He heard the applause. He must have said to himself, 'Who is this tenor with a lute singing old songs in a Greenwich Village basement who can fill Carnegie Hall? If he can do it once, he can do it again. I better go down and catch him.'

"I say he must've said that to himself because three nights later Walter Prude, his right-hand man, walked into the Vanguard with his wife, Agnes De Mille, the dancer, and Sol Hurok, the famous impresario himself.

"The next afternoon in his office, Sol Hurok signed me to a contract to begin touring in 1945. I didn't believe it.

"With Sol Hurok's contract in my pocket, I packed my lute, sold my furniture on Charles Street, and with my wife and two daughters moved out to Aspen, Colorado. And for years, with Aspen as my base of operations, Hurok sent me concertizing all over the land, as far north as Alaska.

"Once you're picked up by Hurok, you'd think you've got it made. But my concert fees at first weren't that high, you know, and Hurok didn't always provide me with a crowded busy concert season. When the bills started to pile up, I'd call you from Aspen and ask you, 'Can you use me for a couple of weeks?' By God, you always could, either at the Vanguard or The Blue Angel. It wasn't three years I worked for you at the Village Vanguard, like you say. It was all of ten years." Dick laughed at the thought.

"Hurok, alas, is gone, and my concert schedule is diminished. I did one in Alice Tully Hall last year. You were there. D'you notice I use a piano accompaniment now? No more lute or guitar.

"I've taken a job teaching the use of the actors speaking voice at The State University of New York at Stony Brook on Long Island to fill time and eat. I sing to my class, tell them how it's done, if such a thing can ever be told.

"Don't be surprised if one of these days one of my students

comes down and asks you for a job. I like to tell my students of my years at the Vanguard, the night Carl Sandburg dropped in, joined me on the floor, and did one of his talking blues. I tell 'em about Woody Guthrie and about Leadbelly's last concert.

"It was 1949, I got a call one day in Aspen from a manager in Omaha, who booked Leadbelly for a series of concerts in the Texas Panhandle. Leadbelly was too sick to go on. Would I go down to Lubbock, Texas, and substitute for him? So with Bonnie, my daughter, I flew down to Lubbock.

"I learned that the night before, they had to carry Leadbelly on stage with the curtains drawn and sit him in a chair so he could do his show. After that performance his wife, Martha, who was on the road with him, decided he'd had it and she wouldn't take no for an answer. She's got to get him back to a doctor in New York. Three months later Leadbelly was dead."

"The audience expecting Leadbelly, got me. So I sang some of his songs for them, songs we used to do at the Vanguard. I told them about Leadbelly—his power, his dignity, his courtliness, how in spite of everything he wasn't consumed with black anger.

"My students also like to hear about the night of the big fight," Dick continued.

"What fight?"

"The night those five sailors walked in drunk."

"Three sailors, Dick."

"No, there were five, I tell you."

"Three, four, or five," I said, "thank God Burl Ives was there that night. Those sailors didn't know what hit 'em."

"When that sailor punched me on the nose," Dick said, "I let go a backhand with my open palm across his Adam's apple. I used to play a pretty good game of tennis, you know."

"Burl was still in uniform, had just been mustered out of the Army."

"Did you know that Burl was a tackle on the University of Illinois football team before he came to New York, and could run a hundred yards in eleven seconds flat?" asked Dick.

"Yeah, those sailors discovered he was no slouch," I said.

"You fought like a demon," said Dick.

"Like a demon, did I? I remember I picked up a chair. That's the first thing I always did when a fight started—pick up a chair."

"A chair is the best defensive weapon in a nightclub fight," Dick agreed. "Leadbelly told me that once. But I didn't have time to pick up a chair. It happened so fast. And then it was over. And we threw those five sailors right out onto the street after the cops walked in."

"Three sailors," I said.

"No, I insist there were five. At least that's how I tell it to my class in Stony Brook. The night of the big fight! Faces on the Barroom Floor I call that night. They love to hear it. A fight in a nightclub."

Dick called for another bottle.

"And now shall I bring you up to date?" said Dick. "I'm about to embark on a project that will take the next five years of my life. It's dynamite! Everything I've done so far, every bloody thing, my ten years at the Vanguard, has prepared me for it: a twenty-four hour taping of the twenty-four books of Homer's *Odyssey*, Fitzgerald's great translation of the greatest of all Greek poems! Thank God I still have the voice for it.

"The National Endowment for the Humanities has granted me one hundred thousand dollars for the first two years of the five-year project. I can start using my own voice again, intoning the ancient, heroic, never forgotten lines of Homer on tape, for posterity. Listen to this."

Dick moved his chair closer to mine.

"Odysseus the Greek warrior," Dick began, "after the siege and sacking of Troy, after twenty years of travel and wandering, returns home to his wife, Penelope, and to Telemachus, his son. Penelope was taking a nap.

"Before he woke her, Odysseus had to slay the suitors who had invaded and violated the sanctuary of his home while he was away. By God, he slew them all. There Odysseus stood. Hear the immortal words of Homer:

> ". . . *spattered and caked with blood*
> *like a mountain lion*
> *when he has gorged upon an ox, his kill*
> *with hot blood glistening over his whole chest*
> *smeared on his jaws, baleful and terrifying*
> *even so encrimsoned was Odysseus*
> *up to his eyes and armpits.*

"Penelope was still napping while this was going on.

"'Do not awaken her,' he ordered his chief female slave. He

learned that two maidservants had gone bad while he was away. They had to be disposed of first.

"And do you care to know how Odysseus disposed of them?" asked Dick. "I've learned this passage by heart:

> *"He tied one end of a hawser to a pillar*
> *and passed the other about the roundhouse top,*
> *taking the slack up, so that no one's toes*
> *could touch the ground. They would be hung like doves*
> *or larks in springes triggered in a thicket,*
> *where the birds think to rest—a cruel nesting.*
> *So now in turn each woman thrust her head*
> *into a noose and swung, yanked high in air,*
> *to perish there most piteously.*
> *Their feet danced for a little, but not long.*

"That's how he disposed of them. It's beautiful," said Dick when he was through. "You always liked the bloody tales, and these are bloody tales aplenty, you old bastard."

"When do you start taping?" I asked him.

"I use a small harp when I'm intoning these immortal lines.

"The way you give the lines and with a harp accompaniment, you can fill Carnegie Hall."

"D'you think so? But maybe I ought to break it in at the Vanguard first. What do you think?"

"I'll make room for you. When I get back to the joint, I'll take a look at my calendar and carve out a couple of weeks for you."

And so we walked out of that restaurant into the New York night, down MacDougal Street, over to Houston and up to West Broadway, looking for another restaurant, and another bottle of wine.

7 : My Move Uptown

I opened The Blue Angel in 1943 on East Fifty-fifth Street, the smart, elegant, rich Upper East Side of Manhattan, and closed it in 1963. It lasted twenty years, a generation.

"How could a place like The Blue Angel close?" people still ask me. In its time it was the greatest nightclub in New York. "There'll never be another place like it," they'd say at three in the morning, when they've had a few drinks under their belt.

It was, indeed, quite a joint while it lasted. For one thing it was decorated in "a smart, continental manner," as the saying goes, by my partner, Herb Jacobi, with the help of Stewart Chaney, the Broadway theater scenic designer. Black patent-leather walls in the bar, tufted grey velour walls with pink rosettes in the main room, banquettes of pink leather, a bright red carpet, black marbletop tables—this was Jacobi's idea of what New Yorkers thought a smart French nightclub looked like. Lenny Bruce didn't like it at all. "Like the inside of a coffin," he said when he worked there.

Over the stage Jacobi had hung a small, blue-tinted Michelangelo angel.

But it wasn't the decorations that made the place so great, it was the acts that appeared there.

I'm often reminded when I pick up a paper, go to the theater, or turn on my TV set, of some of the great and not so great acts that passed through The Blue Angel in twenty years. Many of the performers have changed their acts in the meantime—gone from comedy or song to acting, writing, directing, producing. Others have perfected their old acts. Dorothy Loudon, the star of big Broadway hits *Annie,* and *Sweeney Todd,* began her singing career at The Blue Angel fifteen years ago. When Yul Brynner sat on top of our grand piano the year we opened, playing his guitar and singing Russian folk songs, he gave small inkling of a once and future king. Josephine Premice, who's recently closed a long Broadway run in *Bubbling Brown Sugar*, was singing and dancing at a benefit in her bare feet in Webster Hall on the Lower East Side when I drafted her for the Vanguard and The Blue Angel in 1947.

Elaine May and Mike Nichols, a great comedy team, were an instant success when they opened in 1960, having just arrived in New York as two broke young kids from Chicago. Today Mike is a Broadway director and Elaine, a Hollywood writer.

A lot of great comics played The Blue Angel. Woody Allen made his nervous stand-up debut there when he first cut loose from writing other people's gags. Carol Burnett was a hit in the place in the early fifties. One night a Republican Congressman from Ohio came up from Washington just to hear her sing, "I'm in Love with John Foster Dulles." Wanted to find out if there was anything subversive in the song. "I don't hear anything subversive," he said to me at the bar. "That girl should go places."

Barbra Streisand was a great singer when she opened in the place in 1959. She hardly sings at all in her latest movie. Today she considers herself an actress.

I watched Imogene Coca on Channel 13 the other night, doing a take-off on a tortured torch singer, the same number she used to do at The Blue Angel in 1948. Still funny. But what's Phyllis Diller doing making TV commercials? Besides the money, I mean.

We brought Phyllis to New York from San Francisco—about the same time as Mort Sahl, the first of the angry comics. He's still playing the clubs. But Dick Gregory, whom I found in Chicago, has no time for comedy anymore. When I see *his* name in the papers nowadays, it's because he's been arrested on a picket line.

In 1954 Tom Lehrer took time out from teaching at Harvard to play a month at The Blue Angel, then quit to save his wit for his students. Tom's songs, with their excoriating satire and black humor, used to knock me out.

What you've just read, however, is just a small sampling of The Blue Angel's comic lustre. There are plenty more glittering names to drop: Eddie Mayehoff, Jerry Stiller and Anne Meara, Charlotte Rae, Arte Johnson, Robert Clary, Eartha Kitt, Jonathan Winters, Kaye Ballard, Andy Griffith. Most of these acts went on to fame and fortune, or, like Lenny Bruce, the poor bastard, to fame, fortune, and disaster.

Not every comedian who opened did great at The Blue Angel. Paul Mazursky didn't kill anybody. He's doing all right in Hollywood today, however.

When *Timbuktu!* opened on Broadway and I read the reviews of Eartha Kitt's performance, I remembered a snowy night in February 1947. The snow was knee-high and the wind was howling. At ten o'clock Eartha hadn't yet arrived at The Blue Angel. I phoned her. She wouldn't, couldn't, make it that miserable night—no cabs, no nothing. "The Angel's probably dead anyhow," she said.

"The show's about to go on," I screamed into the phone.

"You'll have to come and get me if you want me to work tonight."

I used to drive a secondhand Olds, the only car I ever owned. I drove up to 147th Street, on Sugar Hill in Harlem, and waited outside her apartment house door until she came down. She got in beside me.

"It's cold in here," she said. "Turn up the heater."

"Don't you have your diamonds to keep you warm?" I tried a joking allusion to Eartha's number that brought down the house every night.

"Turn up the heater," she said.

We drove down Fifth Avenue.

"Why don't you take a night off once in a while?" she said, turning her eyes on me.

"What'd I do with a night off?"

"What'd you do with a night off!" she said mockingly and laughed.

The inside of the car was warm by the time we reached Fifty-fifth Street. It would be nice to take a night off, I kept thinking. Especially a night like tonight, and with this beautiful girl here sitting beside me.

But I didn't even try. I guess I was too dumb.

I caught Portia Nelson in a Soho club the other night, singing as good as she did at The Angel twenty years ago. Maybe better, even. We had a succession of great singers—Evelyn Knight, Maxine Sullivan, Mildred Bailey, Barbara McNair, Miriam Makeba, and Mabel Mercer, the *doyenne* of superclub singers, who today is greater than ever.

Tom O'Horgan, singing and playing a harp, was no great sensation, but he was good for a solid month at The Blue Angel. He soon gave up singing, took up residence at Cafe La Mama, became a director, and went on to turn *Hair* into a million-dollar musical.

Diahann Carrol was a breathtaking eighteen-year-old when she opened in the 1950s. One Monday night last year she came down to the Vanguard to hear Thad Jones. "I've got a daughter who's eighteen," Diahann told me. "Can you believe it?"

Bobby Short wasn't much more than eighteen when Jacobi hired him. I see he's back again at the Carlyle, where the customers seem to think he'll be singing and playing his piano forever.

What year was it you opened at The Blue Angel?" I asked Bobby one night not long ago.

"Never mind what year," he replied. "If I tell you, you'll know how old I am. I never tell my age. Being a black man, The Blue Angel was the only nightclub on New York's upper east side I could've worked at the time. Does that tell you what year it was?

"I started building my following at The Blue Angel. They followed me to the Carlyle, I guess—some of them. Some nights I see the same faces here at the Carlyle I used to see in The Blue Angel bar. I like pleasing people who come to hear me sing. They make requests, push five, ten, twenty dollar bills on me. I never accept tips. Never! But one night a guy flashed a hundred dollar bill on me. He asked for some obscure Cole Porter number— which I knew, of course. I looked at the guy. 'If you lay another hundred on my bass player and drummer,' I told him, 'I might be induced to accept it.' And don't you know, he did. No, I don't accept tips.

"A hundred, two hundred is different, Max. Know what I mean?"

When Bobby left The Blue Angel, we put in Eadie and Rack, a piano team. Since we had to buy a second piano, we could now book other piano teams, like Ferrante and Teicher, who were pretty good. I barely recognized them on TV the other night, with their new beards and hairdos.

Don't get me wrong. I'm not taking bows for discovering all this great talent. What did Jacobi and I actually do? We were there, running a joint. We paid the rent.

We turned down some pretty good people: Cyril Ritchard, Carl Reiner, Ralph Meeker. "They don't have a nightclub act," said Jacobi, and I had to agree with him.

It's the acts that we found or found us that kept the place going for twenty years.

When I met Jacobi in 1942, he was booking acts for the Ruban Bleu on East Fifty-sixth Street. Before emigrating from Paris to New York in 1936, he had booked acts for Les Boeufs Sur Les Toits, a nightclub in Paris. Tall, dark, smooth in his grey pin-striped suit, immaculately barbered, Jacobi is the only man I ever met who looked like a nightclub owner.

I was a Village boy, running a basement in Greenwich Village for eight years, and I saw a chance to move uptown to the big time when Jacobi proposed The Blue Angel to me. It took ten grand to open the place. Jacobi didn't have any money. I skipped paying my liquor bills at the Vanguard one month, went on C.O.D., and thus scraped together five thousand, my share. A friend lent Jacobi his half.

We paid his friend six grand out of The Blue Angel's profits once we opened. It took a year, and for a year Jacobi's Shylock friend and a table of cronies ate dinners in the place, waiting for their money.

This was the good part of our partnership. Jacobi and I never counted our dollars jealously between us. We were careless like that. We never hassled each other over a buck.

On the afternoon of the night we opened, Jacobi handed me an envelope. "Read it when you get a chance," he said. I had a hard time deciphering his crabbed handwriting. He had planned to say these things to me in person but decided at the last minute to write instead. He wanted me to know of his feelings at the moment when we were about to open The Blue Angel's doors, how much he appreciated my forbearance, my giving him a free hand to decorate the place, to book the opening show, every-thing without any interference on my part.

I've kept the letter. Jacobi was more shy and sensitive than I imagined.

I let Jacobi carry the ball because I was a Villager who had come uptown to the Upper East Side of Manhattan, "another world." "Everything north of Fourteenth Street is another world," we used to say in the Village. So I kept my mouth shut.

Jacobi hired a French chef and a French lady whose specialty was making omelettes. She had a repertoire of two hundred of them. I could sit down—on a black leather chair—order "an omelette fines herbs," and have it served up to me by two Italian waiters dressed in tails. I was up there in the big time at The Blue Angel all right.

I learned that an omelette had been served to the Duchess of Windsor one night. The waiters talked about it for a week. And one night I wandered into the kitchen and found the chef and the omelette lady on chairs facing each other, quietly asleep.

Our first partners' quarrel: I said The Blue Angel was for booze and entertainment. Jacobi held out for omelettes and chic. When a nightclub is crowded every night, like The Blue Angel was, partners' quarrels don't matter. And The Blue Angel was crowded every night right from the start.

The opening show consisted of four acts: Mme. Claude Alphand, the wife of the French ambassador, an amateur chanteuse who preferred singing in a nightclub to living in the embassy in Washington; an Ecuadorian baritone who sang strictly Spanish; Brenda Fraser, an arch British comedienne; and Sylvia Marlowe on a harpsichord, playing Bach and boogie.

It didn't take long for The Blue Angel to gain the reputation in show business as the number one showcase in New York for acts that were looking to go places. Managers and agents began knocking on our door submitting their "hot properties"—"great," "terrific," "sensational" acts, "just the acts you're looking for."

So why did we have such a hard time finding the acts we were looking for? I remember we were always looking for an act to replace an act that was leaving.

We held Monday afternoon auditions. How is an act you're hearing cold in the afternoon going to sound in front of an audience at night? It's good to have another opinion to lean on. That's how I began getting into the acts, so to speak. Jacobi and I, after an audition, would put our heads together and come up with a decision.

We agonized over every act we booked. If an act faltered, we worried. If the audience was cold, we felt rejected. If the audience was enthusiastic, we felt redeemed and triumphant.

In 1943, when The Blue Angel opened, Pearl Bailey and Irwin

Corey—"The Professor," "the world's foremost authority"—were heading the show at the Vanguard.

I wondered how Pearl and Corey would do uptown. Would they kill them at The Blue Angel like they were killing 'em every night at the Vanguard? "Go down and catch Pearl and the Professor," I said to Jacobi. "Tell me what you think."

I remember huddling with Jacobi over Pearl, whether to bring her uptown or not. In 1943 you had to think twice before bringing a black woman to the smart Upper East Side of Manhattan. As for Corey, was he too unkempt in his dirty white sneakers, too angry in his comedy style for the rich clientele out for a simple night's entertainment? The Professor was outraged at the corruption and stupidities of the world. Would they laugh at his helpless, Chaplinesque rages uptown like they were doing downtown?

And would folk singers be right for The Blue Angel? Jacobi thought they might be too sober, too chaste, too unworldly for the fast-stepping uptown crowd.

We decided to take a chance.

Pearlie Mae Bailey and then the Professor both made it up to The Blue Angel in 1945 and did as well as they had at the Vanguard. In 1947 Pete Seeger and The Weavers took the trip uptown, as did Burl Ives, Josh White, and later Harry Belafonte and Richard Dyer-Bennet. In time we had the Kingston Trio, the Limelighters, and Alan Arkin with a guitar, singing folk songs. Sometimes The Blue Angel retaliated, sent acts to the Vanguard. Orson Bean, Woody Allen, Mort Sahl, Lenny Bruce. It was the acts that kept The Blue Angel going for twenty years.

But I've been asked it a thousand times—why did The Blue Angel close? One of my interlocutors had an answer to his own question. "Do you remember the Stork and El Morocco?" he said. "They were great places, too, while they lasted. But came the time when the sons of their old customers stopped bringing the daughters of their old customers there. Do you know why? Those rich kids refused to wear neckties like their fathers. And the headwaiter at the door wouldn't let 'em in without one. So they stopped coming. Business dropped and the joints closed."

"Maybe there were other reasons," I offered.

"Sure. Places grow old, customers grow old, owners grow old."

He looked me right in the eye when he said that.

When we opened The Blue Angel in '43, Forty-seventh Street

to Fifty-ninth Street between Park and Lexington was mostly residential. With time the apartment houses came down and office buildings rose in their stead. In the old days, if you lived in the neighborhood, you could go to a Broadway show and walk home, and maybe stop off at The Blue Angel for a late supper and catch a couple of the acts. We used to get a lot of customers like that. That easy metropolitan way of life in New York was changing as the trek to the suburbs speeded up. The neighborhood started looking dark and deserted.

A night out on the town was turning into a big deal. It meant baby sitters, taking a late train home or staying in town overnight. You thought twice before doing it.

And many Blue Angel regulars didn't get around much anymore, couldn't take the late hours, had to get to bed, make that early appointment in the morning. I used to get a lot of talk like that from old customers. As for their sons and daughters, they just didn't go for The Blue Angel like they didn't go for the Stork or El Morocco.

Then there was the onset of television. Television scouts—who called themselves comedy and talk-show talent coordinators—used to haunt The Blue Angel to recruit acts for their shows. The Blue Angel was a cradle, a testing ground, a school readying acts for TV's insatiable appetite.

Somehow, some way, it all began to change. Acts didn't seem to need The Blue Angel any longer to get into TV where the big money was. For instance we found Peter, Paul and Mary—a great act. When we wanted to bring them back three months later, their manager would let them appear only on television, in arenas, or college gymnasiums at thirty-five hundred bucks for a one-night stand. We were priced out.

Finding acts—the kind of acts that set the town talking—was becoming tougher all the time. A pretty good act wasn't enough. It had to be fresh, new, exciting.

My partner Jacobi saw the handwriting on the wall. He looked around and decided he wanted out while there was still time. Not being the "maven" I thought I was, I bought him out for thirty-five thousand cash in 1959. I didn't, I couldn't, believe The Blue Angel had had it. I thought I could keep it alive, find the acts that made it what it always was—the greatest nightclub in New York. It isn't easy to see a place go down the drain. I called in Stewart Chaney to look the place over, freshen it up, give it a new face. Maybe that was what it needed.

But there it was, happening all around me. I didn't see it, didn't want to see it—that a new generation of night prowlers didn't want to go to the kind of place The Blue Angel was. They didn't want to watch an act; they wanted to do their own act. They didn't want to sit glued to a chair in a nightclub. They wanted to do their "own thing," investigate the mystery of the night, listen to a little music, get up and dance maybe, or just sit and talk to the girl sitting next to them at the bar.

Closing night, Jacobi dropped in to sit with me in a corner. At the end I felt strangely relieved, elated even. The Blue Angel had become a burden. The tight little stage had become too tight. If I was ever going to do anything again, it would have to be on another stage. Twenty years, a generation. The show was over. Let the curtain fall. So I closed up and went back to the Village Vanguard, where I came from.

8 : Le Directoire

If you're running a successful nightclub in New York—the place jammed every night, the best entertainment in town, the booze flowing and the money rolling in—why go and open up another place three blocks down the street? We did just that, Jacobi and I, in 1948, five years after we opened The Blue Angel.

We bought the equipment of the defunct Cafe Society Uptown from Barney Josephson for seventy-five thousand. Why we paid Barney all that money when he desperately needed a tenant for his building, I'll never know. As it turned out, we took a good look at the aging stuff he'd left behind and decided to dump it all—chairs, tables, the bar, the kitchen. We decided to strip the joint bare and build from scratch a new nightclub on the premises.

We weren't *entirely* stupid. Jacobi and I weren't opening a place to compete with ourselves at The Blue Angel. This place had to be different. Since it seated three hundred, considerably larger than The Blue Angel, we planned to book bigger acts. What those acts would be we didn't exactly know, beyond the one we had already signed up for the opening: Kay Thompson, Andy Williams, and the Williams Brothers. They were playing in Miami and Walter Winchell was trumpeting them every other day in his column as the greatest act in nightclub history.

"Let's put together a place that'll set this town on its ear," said Jacobi. "We have the money; we have the location; we have the know-how, and we have a great opening act. This place has capacity. We can now pay more money for acts—that is, for acts that demand more money."

One difference between the new place and The Blue Angel: In the new place there would be dancing. After the show a man and his lady could rise, stretch, and dance.

We didn't stop to think that maybe they didn't need to dance, that they didn't want to dance, that a good show was enough. A customer at The Blue Angel once confided to me, "I bring my wife to The Blue Angel often because I don't have to dance with the girl."

But no, we hired Ted Straeter and his band for eighteen hundred a week so that a couple could do the rhumba instead of going home and making room for another couple who'd come to see the show.

What to name the place? We exhausted ourselves trying on names to fit the dimensions of this new joint, a name with promise and resonance, something Continental, of course. Jacobi came up with: Le Directoire. "It has everything I've always wanted in a name," he proclaimed.

I had to look it up in an encyclopedia to find out what the hell Jacobi was talking about.

(The night before we opened, a taxi driver said to me, "How 'n hell am I gonna bring people to your joint if they can't pronounce the name of it?")

Who could be trusted to build and decorate Le Directoire? Jacobi said the man or woman chosen for this important job should be someone who had never decorated a nightclub before. We wanted smart new ideas, none of your tired standard nightclub decor.

Jacob found Bill Pahlmann, the reigning interior decorator of the day, and offered him the job. It was generally agreed that Pahlmann did an outstanding job. The walls were screens of delicately woven threads of pink, silver, and gold, created especially for us by an old lady in a loft on Third Avenue. The carpet, instead of nightclub red, was taupe. The color scheme was subtle and provocative, said the critics, down to the waiters' jackets and the doorman's uniform. I know one thing, I had a hell of a time finding a doorman who'd consent to wear the goddamn uniform designed by Jacobi and Pahlmann to evoke the Directoire period of La Belle France.

Barron Polan, who managed Kay Thompson and the Williams Brothers, dropped in one afternoon to watch the progress Pahlmann and his staff were making. He looked around admiringly, then asked, "But where's the stage? Where're you gonna put the show?"

"On the dance floor, of course," said Jacobi.

"You mean you're gonna put my act in a hole on the dance floor where nobody can see them?" he screamed.

Polan was a mercurial man. For five minutes he raged about the quality of Kay and the Williams Brothers. It was an act that had to be seen as well as heard; an act that needed visibility, elevation, presentation. He wouldn't let them open, contract or no contract, if we didn't provide a stage. On the dance floor they would be lost, wasted.

We told Pahlmann to stop everything until he solved this knotty problem. Pahlmann solved it in a most ingenious way, for five thousand. He built a stage, eighteen inches high, the size and shape of the dance floor, and had it wired so that at the push of a button, it could move and come to rest on the dance floor, and at the push of another button, stand itself up on its side right next to the dance floor. Barron Polan was satisfied.

So there the stage stood, right next to the dance floor; there was no other place for it, silent and waiting for the night when it was to be called on for Kay Thompson and the Williams Brothers to go on.

The trouble was you couldn't seat anybody where the stage stood. It was taking up some of our best ringside seats. The people who should've been sitting there were outside trying to get in. And that didn't put money in the cash register.

So Jacobi told Pahlmann to build and design a small glass-enclosed bar for waiting and refuge, where a couple who had arrived during the show could have a drink and wait for the next one. A good idea, but it just didn't work. That little bar stayed empty all the nine months we were open, except for the bartender, and it ate twenty-five seats of our capacity.

"I came to see the show, not wait for it," was the verdict of disgruntled customers.

On the afternoon of opening night, when we began dressing the room, putting tables and chairs in place, we discovered that we had a lot of tables and chairs left over. We stopped everything so we could take a careful count of our capacity. Every recount came out the same: two hundred twelve seats, no more, no less, but not the three hundred seats we thought we had. Jacobi and I were stunned. "What the hell did Pahlmann do to us?"

"You can't get into the place," people kept telling each other those first weeks. That didn't stop them from trying, Winchell had given Kay and Andy such a powerful buildup.

Arturo, the headwaiter, was besieged, begged, and threatened. The tips he amassed were outrageous. Every seat in the place was paid for twice by people who considered themselves lucky to get in. Arturo opened up a nightclub of his own on Second Avenue a year later with the money that was pushed on him every night during Kay and Andy's ten-week run. Some people didn't make it through the jam at the door. Some were slighted, some felt slighted, some never forgave us. Louis Sobol, the *Journal American* columnist, wouldn't talk to me for ten years.

Ten weeks is not forever. Kay, Andy, and his brothers had to leave for other commitments that Barron Polan had made for them. We put three acts in their place to take up the slack: Les Compagnons des Chansons, eight boys from Paris; Mata & Hari, a brother and sister dance team noted for their prodigious lifts; and Abe Burrows doing comedy songs at the piano, his first professional try in New York. I thought it was a great show, but it wasn't Kay Thompson and the Williams Brothers.

A cab would drive up, the doorman'd open the door, a face'd lean out. "Is that woman, Kay what's her name, and her brothers on tonight?" When given a negative reply, the cab door would bang shut and off they'd drive.

We borrowed acts from The Blue Angel. But even Pearl Bailey couldn't warm up the dwindling audience. The place was too big (it wasn't; it only looked that way), the ceiling too high. Pearl felt remote, in left field, on that massive rectangular stage that Pahlmann had built. Every act we tried felt anticlimactic. Vivienne Segal, who had just closed in *Pal Joey* with Gene Kelly; Muriel Smith, the Carmen in *Carmen Jones*, the toast of Broadway the year before—nothing felt right in the Directoire, nothing except Kay Thompson and the Williams Brothers. The place was made to house them. Nothing else would fit.

Le Directoire was in trouble: Empty tables stood like guilty reminders of something gone wrong.

One night we decided to close the joint and give it back to Barney.

The stage that Pahlmann had built brought a hundred bucks at the auction.

9 : Lenny and Me

Ten years ago, when Lenny Bruce stories were making the rounds, researchers, newsmen, and freelance writers with tape recorders came around to ask me questions about Lenny. What happened to him when he worked at The Blue Angel and the Village Vanguard? I didn't keep any secrets from them, but I guess they didn't ask the right questions because a lot of what happened to him at the Angel and the Vanguard didn't find its way into the articles, books, and plays about him.

Back in 1960 or '61 Lenny had closed at The Den, a room in the basement next to the boiler room in a second-rate hotel on lower Madison Avenue, and he dropped in to see me. I made him an offer: two weeks at The Blue Angel.

Jacobi and I were looking for acts that were different and Lenny Bruce was different—the funniest, angriest, filthiest, most outrageous comic in the country. "America's number one vomic," Winchell called him. Winchell didn't like him.

"Too many straight people come to your joint," Lenny said right off. "What I need is a room of my own in New York, where my kind of people can come to see me—me alone."

But his buddies, advisers, and managers had other ideas: According to them, Lenny had played holes, toilets, creep joints, fag joints, and Mafia-owned joints long enough. It was time he went into a smart, elegant, prestigious room like The Blue Angel.

We discovered after he opened that a lot of The Blue Angel clientele had never heard of him. They came to The Blue Angel "for the show," because "the show is always good." It was "a place to go to." "You can take your wife there." They didn't come to see Lenny Bruce.

So when Lenny started "shpritzing" them with choice obscenities, some people froze. They'd never heard such words used in a nightclub. So they got up, paid their checks, and walked out.

"Who is that dirty-mouthed person?" they'd ask at the door.

Lenny felt the cold draft of their disapproval. He couldn't stand being rejected. "Squaresville" he called The Blue Angel. He hated the decor. He was glad when his two weeks were over and he could go back to Hollywood.

A week later I received a three-page telegram from Lenny. "Forget about The Blue Angel," it said. "I want the Village Vanguard in New York, my kind of place, where my kind of people will come to see me. Get yourself a jazz trio—that's all you need—me and a jazz trio." He wanted thirty-five hundred a week. "I'll work seven nights a week, two shows a night, three shows on Friday and Saturdays. What do I need a night off for? Reserve a room at the Marlton on Eighth Street. Ask 'em to paint it dark blue. And fix up your goddamn dressing room. I'll pay the carpenter."

Two weeks later Lenny opened. He stayed six weeks at the Vanguard.

He was right. He jammed the place every night with his kind of people: college kids, hookers, fags, the jet set, Harlem society, the Broadway and Hollywood crowd. Nobody walked out on him.

Every night when his first show was over, he'd repair to the kitchen followed by a crowd of fans, agents, managers, moochers, record promoters, ghost writers. There he would hold court. Lenny's dressing room was never big enough to hold everybody who wanted to talk to him.

I could never get near him. Besides, I had to keep an eye on the place. With the kind of people he was pulling, you had to keep an eye on everything. In the six weeks of his run, I never got a chance to sit down with Lenny, alone, at a table, never got a chance to talk to him. I regret it to this day.

My nephew Barry, who doubled as the Vanguard's manager and cashier, got to know him better. Barry thought that Lenny was not only the greatest stand-up comic in America, but also a deep thinker, a social and political philosopher, and a great guy. He was proud that Lenny made a buddy of him. Lenny'd call up Barry at eight in the morning, wake him up. He'd have been up all night himself. "Come down and have a cup of coffee with me.

I'm in that all-night deli at Second Avenue and Sixth Street."
Barry'd leave his wife in bed, get dressed, hike down to Second
Avenue, and sit around and talk with Lenny for an hour.

"What did you talk about," I asked Barry one day.

"Everything. His mother, his wife Honey, his kid."

"Was he high? Was he drunk?"

"You know he never takes a drink. That Lenny sees everything," said Barry. "He thinks your waiters aren't hustling drinks
enough."

"He's right," I agreed.

"Then he talked about you. What the hell are you so nervous
about? Walking around as if you were off your nut."

"I'm nervous all right," I said. "I'm nervous about cops in the
place. I don't want to see the joint busted. That's what I'm
nervous about."

"I told him that."

"So what'd he say?"

"Tell Max forget it. There were two cops in the joint last night
taping the show."

"He said that? You're kidding!"

"Lenny can spot cops. They come in pairs and look like Mike,
'that Polish goniff bartender from Canarsie who rips Max off
every night.' That's how he put it."

"How'n hell does he know Mike lives in Canarsie?" I asked.
"So what else does he talk about?"

"He says 'Max has never come up to me once—not once—and
said, Lenny, business is great, and you're great! Not once. He
doesn't dig me.'"

"Do I have to dig every number? Why does he tease cops
when he knows they're in the place taping his show? Ask him
that. Does he have to congratulate them on their fine asses when
they're dressed like dames in pantsuits, parading all around
Times Square as decoys to catch rapists and pimps? Why does he
do it? Ask him that."

"It gets laughs."

"One number that doesn't kill me is his number on snot. Ten
minutes on the subject of snot. I thought about asking him to pull
it, but then I thought I better keep my mouth shut. He wouldn't
do it anyway. No, he's right, I don't dig every one of his
numbers. Take the one where a Jew breaks open a mezuzah. He

finds a piece of paper inside that says, 'Made in Japan—Gevult!'
What's so funny about that?"

"It gets laughs."

"Another Jew opens another mezuzah. This Jew finds a
marijuana joint stashed inside. What's so funny?"

"It gets laughs."

"Then he takes off on rabbis, fashionable reform rabbis and
their sermons, their clipped British accents in the synagogues of
the rich. Suddenly the rabbi forgets himself and reverts to the
shtetl he comes from. 'Danksalot.' What's so funny?"

"Lenny's not an anti-Semite," protested Barry. "He's a Jew
himself."

"Some old customers tell me they don't dig his Yiddishisms.
OK? These are people who were born on Hester Street, made
money, moved to Great Neck, learned to play golf and tennis like
the *goyim*, and are moving back to town now that their children
have grown up. They don't think his Jewish stuff is funny."

"Their kids like him," said Barry. "Lenny's ahead of his time."

"Sure he's ahead of his time. He used 'motherfucker' when you
were still in high school. 'Shit,' 'putz,' 'schmuck'—what does he
need all that horny material for?"

"Words rightly used can be abrasive, curative, shake you up,
make you think. Know what I mean?" (Barry was taking courses
at the New School for Social Research and knew what he was
talking about.)

"I just don't want to see a cop walk in and pull my license off
the wall. And I don't go for his Catholic material either.
Remember, cops are Catholic. Take that number where Oral
Roberts calls up the Pope long distance. "Hello, Johnny boy!
What's shaking, baby? How's the old lady? Cool it, nobody here
knows you're Jewish." How does a cop who's Catholic feel
hearing that kind of stuff in a nightclub?"

"Lenny's not against religion," Barry answered.

"How should those cops know Lenny's not against religion?"

"Sometimes I wonder why you booked Lenny."

"He fills the room, stupid."

In 1961 Lenny Bruce was money in the bank, and he had no
trouble booking himself into nightclubs and concert halls everywhere. Operators and promoters were glad to get him. I brought

him back to the Village Vanguard for two weeks, and he packed the place every night like he did the first time.

Then I began reading stories about him. He was getting busted in nightclubs all over the country: the Alhambra in Los Angeles, the Jazz Workshop in San Francisco, the Gate of Horn in Chicago. It was either obscenity or drugs. He opened in a place called The Establishment in London. The British government barred his return to the British Isles. In Sydney, Australia, the local papers hounded him out of the country after his opening night show, when he told his audience "I'll piss on you."

Then I heard he was back in Hollywood. People who saw him brought back stories about how he was sick, broke, and unable to get any work. Nightclubs were afraid to book him.

It was 1964. I saw an item that Lenny was about to open in a new nightclub on Bleecker Street in the Village: Cafe Au Go Go. I caught his show opening night. He looked fatter, had grown a beard, seemed nervous and more frantic than when he was at the Vanguard. He spent forty minutes talking about his busts, the testimony of the cops, the judges, the prosecuting attorneys, his own lawyers whom he had grown to distrust. From now on, he was going to be his own lawyer, he said.

Once he got into his material, he got the laughs he always did, but he wouldn't stay with it. Off he'd go again about his busts, his debts, how broke he was, how he was about to lose his house in Hollywood. He couldn't stop talking about all this.

I felt like going up to him and saying, "Lenny, forget it. Don't let them do this to you. Don't let them break you. Stick to your material. Do your material. You're a comedian—a great comedian." But Lenny wasn't a guy you could tell anything to.

Three days later I read that the cops walked into Cafe Au Go Go and busted him for giving an obscene performance. I didn't think he'd ever get busted in New York.

How did it happen that he was never busted at the Vanguard? I often ask myself that question. I guess I was lucky.

10 : Meet Joe Glaser, Agent

Joe Glaser was the most obscene, the most outrageous, and the toughest agent I've ever bought an act from. I got into the habit of dropping in on Joe to talk, to see what was happening.

"Max," he began on one of these visits, "I've got a girl for you. She's a star already. You can make her a real star. But I warn you, I'm not gonna bring her down to one of your goddamn afternoon auditions. I've been down to one of your auditions. Once is enough. You turned Anita O'Day down, remember? Oh, yes you did. Sure, you used Anita later on. I know all about that. But it took you a year to make up your mind.

"Listen to me, this girl's been knocking around a lot of dinky rooms for years, and nothin's happening. She needs a room like yours, where she can spread her talent. Know what I mean? Rightly presented, this girl'll make you a fortune. Listen to what I'm saying."

He snapped on his intercom and shouted at the top of his voice, "Bert! I got Max Gordon here. Bring me a couple of Dinah's latest records.

"Tell you what I'm gonna do," Joe began, and by this time Bert had brought in a couple of records and was handing them to Joe. "You know Max, Bert." We nodded. Joe handed me the records, and I glanced at the jackets. *Dinah Washington Sings the Blues*. "Take 'em with you, Max. They're yours. Bert, sit down a minute. I want you to hear what I'm saying to Max. Max," he boomed at me, "Dinah Washington will make you a fortune! Am I right, Bert?" Bert nodded a silent assent.

"Take those records down to your place and listen to 'em. I want your room for her. And I don't care about the money! Bert, what did you get for Dinah in that vershtunkene hole in Detroit? Fifteen hundred a week? Is that right, Bert?" Bert nods another assent. "But I'm not asking you for that kind of money. You listen to those records, and I'll call you in two days." Joe wasted no time.

Joe had started out managing heavyweight fighters in Chicago in the Twenties, and he never got over the manner and style of his Chicago days, even after he took over the management of Louis Armstrong and moved to New York, where he built up an independent talent agency with branches all over America and in Europe. He still managed some fighters: He booked Sugar Ray Robinson as a dancer. He was tough, but we always got along. He proved to be right more often than wrong, and in the end I learned to like him.

He once lent me ten grand when I sorely needed it. "No interest, Max. Pay me back when you have it." That was Joe.

Joe was always hopping a plane to visit his ailing mother in Miami, and once I asked Bert, "Does Joe have a wife?"

"He's got a wife . . . in Cleveland," said Bert.

One July I drove with Joe to the Newport Jazz Festival in his air-conditioned Cadillac. Six of us met in the hotel dining room for dinner, Joe's guests. You had to be his guest. Joe wouldn't have it any other way. He surveyed the room, looked at the menu, and motioned the waitress over to the table. Looking her in the eye, he said at the top of his voice, "Young lady, you take care of me, I'll take care of you." Joe liked to have things understood at the outset.

I saw Joe at his office about a month after Dinah Washington opened at the Vanguard and I had picked up the second two-week option. When he saw me through his open door, he shouted my name and ordered me inside.

"I want to talk to you," he cried. "Didn't I tell you, didn't I tell you she'd do it for you, Max? You listen to me. That Dinah! She's something! Is she crowding the room? I know, you don't have to tell me. You nightclub owners'll never give me a straight answer."

He switched on his intercom and shouted into it so his voice reverberated through the whole floor. "Bert! Come in here for a minute!"

Bert walked in meekly and sat down as ordered.

"I want Max to hear what's going on, what's been happening. I want you to tell him what that fat broad who runs that toilet down in Miami, what she offered me for Dinah after she got the word about how Dinah is packing the Vanguard. Twenty-five hundred dollars! Is that right, Bert?"

Bert nodded compliantly.

"I swear to you on my mother's deathbed that I'm telling you the truth. You got her for a grand. But I want her to stay in your joint. I told you I'd give you all the options, you know. And I meant it. I want Dinah in New York. I want the critics to hear her again. I want to freshen her career. I want to get her a new record contract. Am I right, Bert? I'll take less money now for more money later.

"Bert, go ask Izzy to run out for a couple containers of coffee."

Bert slunk out. Joe took about six phone calls that were waiting for him. In walked Izzy carrying a paper bag. Izzy was a slight, sixtyish man with steel grey hair whom I usually saw sitting in the corridor when I dropped in on Joe. Joe had two or three of these old-timers around, show biz retirees Joe knew in the old days whom he kept on his payroll to run errands.

While Joe was fumbling with the coffee and the Danish pastry that Izzy had set down before him, I figured it was a good time for me to tell him what I had come to see him about. It had happened the week before, at the first show after Dinah was introduced. She came out of the dressing room into the spotlight and as the applause died down and she was about to go into her opening number, I noticed that she was wearing a blond wig. I couldn't believe it—a stupid-looking blond wig. Nobody laughed, but that was only because of the innate good taste of the Village Vanguard audiences. I told Joe that I was so upset by this vision of a blond wig on Dinah Washington's head that I had to see him. And that wasn't all.

"A blond wig!" shouted Joe.

"Yes, a blond wig!" I shouted back. "Here's a handsome black woman, a great singer, a star, and she comes out—I didn't believe my eyes—with a blond wig sitting on top of her head."

"These *schwarzes* are nuts," said Joe. "She's got herself a new guy; that's what it is. Otherwise why should she put a blond wig on her head? She's got a new guy taking her money. Let me give you some advice, Max. Don't pay it any attention. Make believe you don't see it. She'll get over it. I know Dinah.

"She'll dump this guy, whoever he is. And the blond wig will go away. As long as business holds up, what've you got to worry about? And another thing, you think it's undignified, you think it's grotesque. But I'll bet you some fancy customers are quietly getting a kick out of the sight of a blond wig on a black broad."

Joe shouted some obscenity-laden instructions to his secretary.

"And that's not all, Joe," I continued when things quieted down. "Dinah has caught a bad cold, but such a cold that for the last three nights, she hasn't been able to do her shows. And I don't know, should I exercise my next option or not?"

"What d'you mean? You tell me the place is crowded, and you tell me Dinah ain't doing her shows. If she ain't doing 'em, who's doing 'em?"

I gave Joe the cold facts, how every night Dinah came down to the Village Vanguard dressed in her evening gown and with her came another girl singer dressed in another evening gown, driven down by a guy in a Cadillac who waited outside in front of the place all night.

The show goes on. Introducing Dinah Washington! Dinah comes out in her blond wig, starts the opening number and manages to finish it. She then introduces this little girl who takes over and does four, five numbers. Then Dinah comes back and together they bow off.

Joe looked at me as if I couldn't possibly be telling the truth.

"Who's the singer? Is she good? Is she pretty?"

"Gloria Lynne. She's good and she ain't bad looking. But she ain't Dinah Washington. The people come down to hear Dinah Washington. They're not coming down to hear Gloria Lynne."

"So. Are you getting any complaints?"

"Joe, I got to admit there's not been that many complaints. But how long can this go on? If Dinah ain't going to do the shows, the people are going to find out and stop coming. My question is: Do I exercise my next option on Dinah when Dinah ain't going to, or can't, make it? Nobody's even heard of Gloria Lynne."

"Max! I'm coming down to your joint tonight to see for myself what's going on, even though I hate nightclubs. I don't drink, and I'm in bed every night at ten o'clock."

I knew this for a fact. Joe liked to get home to his apartment on West Fifty-fifth Street, where he lived alone except for the prize-winning dogs that he showed in Madison Square Garden. Never talked much about them, but I heard they won ribbons, and he liked to get home early enough to spend some time with them.

But Joe was all business now. "Max, I got to go down and see for myself. What's this girl's name again? Gloria Lynne?"

Joe snapped on his intercom and shouted into it. "Bert, we're going down to the Village Vanguard tonight. Do you hear? There's a girl down there, Gloria Lynne. Max says she's good. Maybe you can sign her. Do you hear? Max, don't do nothing until you hear from me."

At this point his secretary walked in to tell him that a man from the State Department was on the phone.

"What the fuck does he want?" Joe growled as he took the call. "They want to send Louis to Africa, Max," he said hanging up. "But if they want Louis Armstrong, they're gonna have to pay him. I'm not gonna send Louis no five thousand miles for peanuts, even for the State Department." He paused, then roared at his secretary, "Did you send Lucille that check?" Turning to me he said, "That's Louis's wife."

I once heard that Joe collected all of Louis's earnings and paid him a thousand—or was it two thousand—a week, whether Louis worked or not. And, the story went, he also paid Louis's divorced wives their alimony every week. Lucille, I believe, was his fifth.

"Max, Louis sold a million records of 'Mack the Knife.' I just got the figures this morning. And he didn't want to make it, didn't think the song was right for him. I told him, 'Louis, it's right for you.' It's a good thing he listens to me." He paused briefly.

"Now you listen to me, Max," he shouted. "I'll be down tonight. I've got to see Dinah in that blond wig for myself and get rid of that guy with the Cadillac she's messing around with. We'll see. Don't make up your mind about anything. Wait till you hear from me."

I saw Joe three months after Dinah closed at the Vanguard. "Don't ask me what happened to Dinah's blond wig," he said to me, shaking his head as if he preferred to forget it. "She married the guy with the Cadillac."

11 : Always Get a Piece of the Action

"Like I'm telling you, if you'd signed them in the beginning when they came to you, all those acts, unknown, unemployed, raw, hungry acts—if you'd got a piece of the action right in the beginning—then, when they got to be stars, celebrities, you'd be on easy street today, collecting ten percent of their paychecks and living like a king. Know what I mean?"

It was my friend Jim talking. I hadn't seen him in twenty years. He made a fortune in plastics. He used to be a regular when he was a student at N.Y.U. and Wally Cox was working at the Vanguard in 1947. I remember he was crazy about Wally Cox.

"Look at the names you found, or they found you—what'd it matter? Judy Holliday, Harry Belafonte, Comden and Green, Pearl Bailey, Woody Allen, Barbra Streisand, Mike Nichols and Elaine May, Jerry Stiller and Ann Meara. I could go on. You turned 'em into stars! You made 'em famous! But what good did it do you? You didn't have a piece of the action.

"All right, you paid Wally peanuts. You thought you were getting a bargain. When he graduated from your joint and went on television, when he was cast as Mr. Peepers in that television series that ran for years, you were left out in the cold. Why? Because you didn't sign him up at the start, when he was still an unknown and needed you."

Jim had a way of worrying me.

"It wasn't so easy," I said to Jim.

I remember the afternoon Wally walked into the Vanguard. Wally looked like a high school kid—open shirt, glasses, as if he might be a choirboy in the church around the corner.

84

When I was in high school.

A night off—at home with
my wife and daughters.

Above: That's the Revuers, four of them *(left to right)*: Adolph Green, Judy Holliday, Betty Comden, and Alvin Hammer. They look so young and handsome. This is how they looked, just coming in off the street in their street clothes—rehearsing or auditioning. Judy was so beautiful, and they were all nice kids.

Right: The Revuers onstage. Left to right, it's Judy, Betty, Alvin, and Adolph. They're doing a piece called "A Night in Philadelphia": "Gondolas gliding while we're side-by-siding, / On a night in Philadelphia."

Judy and me.

A Monday night jam session at the Vanguard in 1942. From left to right, Dizzy Gillespie, Harry Lim (who ran the sessions), Vido Musso, Billy Kyle, Cootie Williams, Charlie Shavers, and Johnny Williams. Some Mondays as many as twenty musicians showed up; Monday was their night off from other gigs. And they'd jam 'til four, five in the morning. I paid Harry; he paid them. How much of a bite they got out of the money I paid Harry, I never knew.

Above: John Coltrane: one of the great innovators in jazz! Set a style on his horn that influenced a generation of tenor saxophone players. A hallowed name in jazz. The last place he played before he died was the Village Vanguard. I keep a picture of him on the wall of the place. People are always offering to buy it. They can't buy it.

Left: Miles Davis when he was a kid. This is how he looked when he came to New York, playing for the first time in the big city. That's Roy Haynes on drums behind him.

Pearlie May Bailey in 1943. She sang the blues when she started at the Vanguard. Gave up the blues for comedy and developed into one of the funniest comediennes in the business. Appeared at The Blue Angel and Le Directoire. She can still sing the blues when the feeling is upon her.

Errol Garner *(left)* and Art Tatum *(right)*, two of the greatest jazz piano players I know, sitting at a piano. Some cat with a camera caught this historic shot. When Errol came to the Vanguard on Monday nights, before you knew it, he was up there sitting in with the band, and they wouldn't let him off. In the 1940s Art Tatum was at Cafe Society Downtown, and during intermissions his bass player would walk Art (who was blind) up to the Vanguard to catch Eddie Heywood. Eddie was no slouch of a piano player himself. Art'd sit there in the dark listening to Eddie, his hands busy playing with the small steel ball bearings he always carried with him.

Dinah Washington in 1949. She could be funny when introducing her songs. What the hell did she say that gave Tallulah Bankhead *(right)* such a kick?

When you think of jazz, you think of Miles Davis. With him here is Coleman Hawkins on saxophone. This was taken about thirty years ago. Miles is still around. He's not doing very much. People are always asking me, what happened to Miles? Why doesn't he play anymore? I don't know what happened to Miles. Poor Coleman, of course, is dead. He was one of the great ones. Here he is, probably playing *Body and Soul,* his number.

Miles Davis on trumpet, Charlie Parker on alto sax, and Max Roach on drums in the early fifties. Who're on bass and at the piano? A quintet like that would have them standing in line today.

Miles Davis in different company: Percy Heath on bass, Roy Haynes on drums and Charlie Parker on alto sax. Charlie is dead now. Percy has a quintet of his own with his brother Jimmy on tenor saxophone. Roy fronts a quartet he calls the Hip Ensemble. Miles is holed up in his house on West Seventy-Seventh Street in New York City. Doesn't touch his trumpet anymore, I'm told. Sits and plays an organ—can you believe it?

Left: Richard Dyer-Bennet. Dick is still at it after all these years—his love affair with the Vanguard. He started there in the forties, and most recently appeared at the place in 1980, intoning Robert Fitzgerald's great translation of the epic tales of Homer's *Odyssey*.

Below: Richard Dyer-Bennet *(far right)* introducing me *(far left)* to Sol Hurok, the impresario, and Agnes DeMille, the famous dancer and choreographer. There's the old mural in the background. I notice the Vanguard used white tablecloths in those days.

Leadbelly was at the Vanguard in 1940. He came back again and again. People'd call up and ask for him. "Is that Mr. Belly still in your place?" a female voice once asked me over the phone. "I hear he's wonderful."

Josh White was a mean singer of the blues, and a great blues guitarist. He was the kind of man who engaged the attention of the ladies—a great ladies' man. He sang to them, and they felt it. He was a great admirer of Leadbelly, considered Leadbelly his teacher. They worked together a lot. At one time Josh teamed up with Libby Hollman. She was a musical-comedy star who wanted to sing blues, so naturally she came to Josh White to learn. He played for her and she sang, and they sang together. Later I think she went off in other directions. Josh of course stayed with the blues. Someone once said Josh wanted to be the Joe Louis of the blues guitar. And he was.

Woody Guthrie taking it easy. No sweat!

photo Harold Leventhal Management Inc.

The Weavers, the daddy of all folk-singing groups. From left to right: Pete Seeger, Lee Hays, Ronnie Gilbert, and Fred Hellerman. The F.B.I. and the House Un-American Activities Committee didn't like some of their songs. But "Good Night, Irene" sold a million and a half records. You can't argue with that.

Above: Twentieth-anniversary party for the Vanguard, 1955. Laughing along with Judy Holliday is Betty Comden. I'm up there somewhere. "Professor" Irwin Corey, "the world's foremost authority," is on the bandstand entertaining the guests.

Right: Peter, Paul & Mary. I used a lot of folk-singing groups after The Weavers in 1949: The Kingston Trio, The Limelighters, Alan Arkin and The Tarriers, The Duke of Iron and His Calypsonians. Then I brought in Peter, Paul & Mary. Their money came up so fast I couldn't bring them back. They had a tough agent.

What's Harry Belafonte singing? I made him a star in the 1950s. After he left the Vanguard and Blue Angel he formed his own company. I had brought Miriam Makeba, the South African singer and dancer, from London to New York in 1960. Harry and MCA, his agency, stole her from me, put her in his own company—and for years they were concertizing all over the world. Harry drops into the Vanguard every once in a while to see the old place. There're no hard feelings between us— no sweat.

A birthday party for Count Basie, Christmas, 1959. Here's the Count himself wearing the bathrobe his men gave him on the occasion. Yessir! Behind him, from left to right: Frank Wess, Al Grey, Eddie Jones, Eddie Green, Frank Foster, Charlie Foulkes in the back, then Benny Powell, and Marshall Royal. That's Thad Jones's smile in the back, then Joe Newman, and Snooky Young. Most of these men are no longer with the Count. I know, because most of them have played at the Vanguard over the years with bands of their own.

An old jazz mural. That's Louis Armstrong on my right, and Bessie Smith on my left.

Gene Cook

Thelonious Monk—the Great Monk. With his hat on. He always kept his hat on when he played. When the other musicians in his quartet were soloing, he'd stand up and jig about the piano. That was Monk all over. One of the most original stylists on the jazz piano, and a great composer. "Round About Midnight" is one of the most popular jazz songs ever written.

Milt "Grooves" Jackson played twenty years with the Modern Jazz Quartet as a side man, the first time at the Vanguard in 1955. For years his fans advised him, "Split, man, and start a quartet of your own." It took him twenty years to make up his mind to leave the Modern Jazz Quartet.

Is there a greater jazz guitarist than Jim Hall? There's always room for disagreement. He was doing a week at the Vanguard back in '64, the week he married his wife, Jane. The ceremony was in the morning, the wedding dinner in the afternoon in a restaurant with a few friends. Jim and Jane hurried to Jane's apartment. They didn't have a lot of time. Jim was due at the Vanguard for his first set at ten P.M. He just made it, with Jane breathless behind him, some of the wedding rice still in her hair.

Betty Carter, of course, is today right on top of the heap. I remember her when she was just sort of getting going. I gave her a job maybe eighteen years ago, and I didn't use her again for about twelve years. Why? At that time I was running The Blue Angel, and I used to come down to the Vanguard late to check out the place, count the money, see if the joint was still there. I happened to walk in on her last show. It was late, it was February, the snow was on the ground; there was nobody in the joint. And there she was, singing to a lot of empty chairs and tables. I could never get that picture out of my mind. She used to come around, looking for work. "Let's wait and see," I'd say. Then finally she said, "You should hear me again, hear me somewhere else, hear me in a place other than the Vanguard. So I went all the way up to Harlem to hear her at a place called Wells's. I heard her, and put her to work. And today she's Betty Bebop, the greatest bebop singer of them all. And do you know what? I can't afford her anymore; she now sings in arenas and does concerts in college gymnasiums. But she comes down to see me. We sit in the kitchen and talk.

Arnett Cobb, a great old-timer, on the tenor saxophone. He makes his home in Houston, Texas, but he comes up once a year to the Vanguard, and the people come out to hear him. Used to play with the big bands. Now he's playing with his own quartet. A great, deep sound if ever there was one.

Brian McMillen

Brian McMillen

Art Blakey, the great bebop drummer. He's had all kinds of groups over the last thirty years. He's constantly refreshing, renewing his group. The last time he played here he brought in a lot of young kids I'd never seen before.

Sonny Rollins when he was
young, about twenty years
ago, before he went to India
and started meditating.

Horace Silver, a great bebop
pianist. He's worked in the
place once every year for
twenty-five years. He makes
his home in California, puts a
new quintet together every
year. He saves a week in his
schedule for the Vanguard. I
had to find a week for him
this year, move other people
around, because I wouldn't
ever want to miss Horace
Silver's playing at the place.

photo by Carol Friedman

The Jones Brothers: *(left to right)*, Hank (who plays piano), Elvin (drums), and Thad (trumpet). What a trio! But they never play together—each has led a combo of his own at the Vanguard. They play sometimes in Japan, Russia, Sweden, at festivals in Nice, Helsinki— they're everywhere. Here one night they ran into each other backstage. Never heard such hooting and hollering.

The disarray in the Vanguard kitchen on a night when a "Live at the Village Vanguard" record is being cut. Terumasa Hino, the trumpet player, is looking for his mouthpiece. The kitchen is normally my office, and the green room where all business is conducted.

photo by Carol Friedman

Archie Shepp Collection

Above: That's old Charlie Mingus himself *(left)* talking to Rahsaan Roland Kirk. Rahsaan came from Columbus, Ohio. When he got to New York, Mingus gave him his first job. They remained friends for life.

Left: Professor Archie Shepp. Archie is a professor of jazz at the University of Massachusetts in Amherst—has been since 1972. Archie has tenure, his wife informed me. He plays a tenor saxophone but he doesn't teach it. He teaches courses, including one in jazz music, in the Black Studies program. During vacations and holidays he'll take a gig playing his horn at the Vanguard.

Lionel Hampton. On September 23, 1977, I produced Dexter Gordon's (no relation) first concert in Avery Fisher Hall in New York's Lincoln Center. Lionel Hampton, a close friend of Dexter's, had played with him in their early California years, when they were just getting started. "I'm going to be in Dexter's first concert," Lionel said to me, "and I'm going to play my vibraphone—whether you hire me or not." He was, and he did. He didn't expect any money, and I didn't pay him any. "Just pay for the cartage of Lionel's vibraphone," his manager told me.

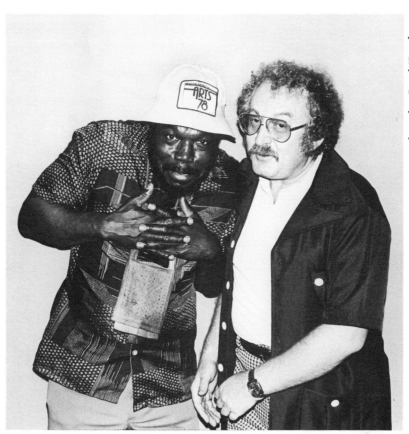

photo by Carol Friedman

Above: Thad Jones *(left)* and Mel Lewis *(right)*, the leaders of our Big Band. Fifteen years of Monday nights! And they're still there at the Village Vanguard every Monday night. Except Thad. He's in Copenhagen leading a big band there. Thad Jones! Come home!

Left: The first time Bill Evans played the Vanguard, twenty-five years ago, he was the intermission piano player opposite the Modern Jazz Quartet. When the MJQ was on, the crowd, who'd come to hear them, was quiet. When Bill took over, a buzz started 'round the room. Who in hell is Bill Evans? They'd never heard of him. He was filling space between sets for the star attraction. Today, Bill is the star attraction. He plays at the Vanguard four, five times a year. Now when he's on, the Vanguard is Town Hall.

A jazz festival on the South Lawn of the White House, June 18, 1978. That's my wife, Lorraine, next to Jimmy Carter. I believe he honestly digs jazz music. He told us that when he was a plebe at Annapolis he used to come to the Village on weekends to hear some jazz. I don't know if he ever hit the Village Vanguard. I didn't ask him.

There's Dexter Gordon on tenor sax and Woody Shaw on trumpet, a great team, on New Year's Eve, 1979. Dexter, after living for sixteen years in Copenhagen, came back to New York, took up his career here, and became a star. One of the greatest attractions in jazz today, Woody is getting along all right, too. They're both recording for CBS. We've had them here at the Vanguard on New Year's Eve three years running. Radio station WRVR does a live broadcast. Well, you know what New Year's Eve is like in a nightclub in New York. And with those two men leading a band, it's *real* lively. We don't hand out any horns to the New Year's Eve celebrators, because we've got men up there blowing their own horns.

photo by Carol Friedman

Me, taking care of business.

Was I looking for a comic, he wanted to know. He heard I was in the market for a comic. Sure I was looking for a comic. I was always looking for a comic in those days.

"I'm a comic," he said.

The Vanguard was empty, unswept, chairs on tables, the smell and smoke of the night before still hanging in the corners. I asked the porter to turn off the two hundred-watt work-lamp and turn on the wall lights. I didn't want to embarrass the kid, expose him to a hot white light so early in the day, with only the two of us in the place.

"Just stand up there and let me hear some of your stuff," I said. "Take it easy, talk it, don't perform it. What's your name again?"

"Wally Cox," he said.

"And what do you do?"

"I'm a silversmith. I work in a shop on West Fourth Street."

"I mean what numbers do you do?"

"Numbers about people I know," he said. "My sixth grade teacher, my sister's boyfriend, my Boy Scout leader, the bully on the block." He did a few.

"What else do you do?"

"Dufo."

"Who's Dufo?"

"He's my best friend."

He did Dufo. Then he did a number about a woman who came into the silver shop where he worked to order a wedding ring for herself. She was living with this guy for two years and felt she needed a wedding ring. It was kind of funny.

"OK. So what else do you do?"

"I do a number about the girl I took to the high school prom. And once I had a summer job in the corner grocery. I do an interview with the owner and his wife. They want to know if I'm honest enough to fill the exacting role of an errand boy. D'you want to hear it?"

I did, and it made me laugh. I wanted to hear more, but I told him I didn't want to keep him too long, that I had worked him more than enough already.

"Sit down next to me, Wally," I said, which he did. "How about coming in next Tuesday at nine? I'll pay you sixty a week, and let's see what happens."

No, don't give them notice at the silver shop, I told him, not yet. Let's see what happens. He promised to be down at nine sharp on Tuesday. No agents, no managers, no signed contracts. It was my word that I wanted him and his promise to be at the Vanguard on Tuesday night.

"It'll be my first job in a nightclub," he said.

He accented "club" when saying "nightclub." That's a laugh already, I thought.

"Have you ever been in a nightclub before?"

"No."

"Watch it, don't get sleepy."

I sat for a moment wondering if Vanguard audiences would dig Wally Cox. It was weird stuff for a nightclub, but he made me laugh. Maybe he'd make other people laugh. The next time Wally auditions anywhere, I thought to myself, I'll bet he'll do a number about his first audition for a job in a nightclub and the negotiations with the boss that followed. I'll bet he'll make it funny. It *was* kind of funny.

"Now what was I supposed to do?" I asked Jim. "Call in a lawyer and tie the kid up? A piece of the action? I didn't even know I wanted him!"

Jim shook his head in disbelief.

"There were times, I suppose, I could've scared a new act I was hiring into signing away a piece of his future earnings to me—if I'd thought about it. But a lot of acts came to me signed to managers or agents who were already taking ten, fifteen, twenty percent of their money. What was I supposed to do?" I asked Jim.

"I guess I just wasn't a ten percentnik."

"You were not only *not* a ten percentnik, you weren't even a one percentnik."

I tried explaining to Jim that after hearing an act and trying to make up my mind whether I liked it or not, and then coming to grips with some manager on the problem of how much to pay that act—I'd had it. It used to exhaust me.

"For instance—let me tell you about a manager by the name of Jack Rollins," I began. When Jack began to sell me Harry Belafonte, he kept telling me how handsome Harry was. "The women go crazy," said Jack.

I told Jack, "There are a thousand good-looking dudes singing in nightclubs in New York who can't sing."

Jack was hurt. "I'm not saying he's handsome because he can't sing. He sings like a sonofabitch."

Harry was handsome all right. At The Blue Angel live audition he sang three numbers and bowed off to light, scattered applause. That was pretty much my reaction, too. A handsome black man singing three pop tunes—not bad, not good. It didn't light any fires in the audience. That was the end of Harry Belafonte, I thought. But I didn't know Jack Rollins.

A month after the audition I got a call from Jack. He had a new singer and he'd pick me up in a cab. He wanted the audition to take place at the Vanguard, not The Blue Angel. He wanted me to hear this singer in the atmosphere this singer belonged in.

"The Blue Angel was a mistake, a nightmare. It was my fault," he said.

"For God's sake, who's the singer and what's The Blue Angel got to do with it?"

"Don't get mad. It's Harry Belafonte."

"Are you crazy? I heard the bastard last month."

"You didn't hear him. I mean you didn't really hear him. Forget you ever heard him. Harry isn't for The Blue Angel, he belongs at the Vanguard."

I told Jack it wasn't necessary for Harry to dress for the audition. Jack said it was. Jack stage-managed everything, told the porter to stop sweeping, asked me where to turn out the lights and turn on the spot. He got up on a chair and inserted a piece of amber gelatin in the spot. He asked me to sit down at a particular table.

The pianist took her place at the piano.

Out came Harry, followed by three male singers, who lined themselves up behind him.

"What the hell does he need those guys for?" I whispered to Jack. "I'm auditioning *him*—him alone—a single, not a chorus." I didn't know then that one of them would turn out to be Brock Peters, but it wouldn't have mattered.

"Backup singers," Jack explained. "To set Harry off, so you can really hear what Harry sounds like, gauge his quality."

Harry went into his first number, "Take This Hammer," a Leadbelly song. (Leadbelly used to do it at the Vanguard every night.) So Jack's making a folk singer out of this guy, I thought. Harry's no Leadbelly, no prisoner swinging a hammer on a chain gang down in Georgia. But he made me listen anyway.

I felt Jack watching me. Harry announced the next number, a calypso. Left arm uplifted, right hand on navel, Belafonte moved his hips as if he were dancing with some imaginary broad.

I hate a phony Caribbean accent. I've had the real thing at the Vanguard—Calypso singers from Trinidad: the Lion, Attila the Hun, King Radio, Macbeth the Great. What the hell am I going to do with a phony Caribbean accent?

It wasn't bad, however. It wasn't good, either. Harry was gathering his breath for the next number: a work song, a work song from Jamaica, "The Banana Song," men loading bananas on a ship. I'd heard that one before. Some years earlier a native girl from Jamaica, Laura Bennett, used to sing it at the Vanguard. She wrote it. As he sang, Belafonte was sweating, really loading bananas on that ship for "Yankeeland."

"Want to hear anything else?" Jack asked me at the end of the number.

I didn't think I wanted to hear *anything* else, but Jack was waiting for me to say something. I didn't know what to say, so I said nothing. The silence was heavy. I got up and moved to another table. Jack followed me.

I began with a comment about Harry's unbuttoned maroon shirt. "Everyone knows he's got a navel."

"The women go crazy," Jack replied.

"You got him singing folk songs. I never heard a folk singer accompanied by a piano. Why don't you teach him to play a guitar?"

"You want a guitar? I got a guitar player, a great guitar player. Knows Harry's material cold." Jack sniffed my interest.

"I don't know if I want him with a guitar or without a guitar. He's stolen all his material. He didn't sing one original song."

"Singers are always stealing from other singers. So what? When Harry does them, he makes them his own."

"What else does he do?"

"Let Harry tell you," said Jack, calling Belafonte to join us.

Belafonte seemed taller as he walked over. We shook hands. Yes, he was feeling great, rehearsing every day, still running that hamburger joint on Grove Street to support his wife and kid. He called off a dozen folk songs he'd been rehearsing.

"He'll fill your room," Jack kept whispering as Harry went to the checkroom to get dressed.

"I'll tell you what I'll do. I'll give him two hundred a week. You pay the guitar player. Four weeks with two four-week options, a fifty-dollar increase with every option I exercise, to be played at the Vanguard or The Blue Angel, wherever I want him."

Jack stuck out his hand. We had a deal, we shook hands. Thank God we had a deal. Thank God it was over. Finished.

Belafonte was right for the Vanguard, as Rollins said, and right for The Blue Angel. I still don't like his unveiled navel. And another thing: When I see Harry nowadays down at the club or at a benefit, I'm still curious—or maybe jealous is the word—about the way he keeps those pants up, with no belt, no suspenders, and no belly.

Anyhow, that was how I hired Harry Belafonte—it's one way of hiring an act.

"And what would you have wanted me to do, start all over again?" I asked Jim. "Get into a shouting match with Jack Rollins about three percent? And furthermore, once Harry Belafonte became a star, he dumped Jack Rollins—contract or no contract."

It was always happening to Jack. He'd bring me an act, and when the act became famous, they'd dump him. It happened like that too with Mike Nichols and Elaine May. Jack had paid their fare from Chicago to New York, auditioned them in the afternoon in the Russian Tea Room over beef stroganoff, and called me.

I gave Mike and Elaine a spot on one of the Sunday night live auditions. The response was so tremendous, we offered them a job starting the next night. Once they opened, Hollywood and Broadway scouts didn't lose any time. This brilliant comedy duo was chock-full of talent. They could write, act, direct, work together or separately. Hollywood and Broadway didn't know exactly how to use them, but they knew they wanted them and they were ready to sign contracts and put money on the line. This was heady stuff for a couple of kids just a few months out of Chicago.

It was Alexander Cohen, the Broadway producer, who eventually presented Nichols and May in concert and put them on Broadway. Jack lost Mike and Elaine, and so did The Blue Angel. Why they didn't let Jack keep handling them, let him talk to Broadway and Hollywood on their behalf, I don't know. I asked Jack about it, about whether he felt any bitterness, and he told me, "When an act is unhappy, when it sulks, when it feels frustrated, the best thing to do is tear up the contract and let 'em go. I'm not sore. I got no time for grudges."

"No wonder Jack didn't have any time for grudges," I explained to Jim. "He had just added a new act to his stable he was crazy about—Woody Allen. Jack wanted me to meet him."

When my partner Jacobi and I came down stairs at The Blue

Angel, we saw a kid with glasses and uncombed hair sitting at a table. The kid got up as Jack introduced us. He was a short, frightened kid with a weak handshake.

"Meet Woody Allen," said Jack.

We all sat down. "This kid is a writer," Jack began. "He writes the most brilliant comedy material in New York. But what does he do with it? Gives it away. That is, he sells it for peanuts to other comedians who are making a fortune out of it—Sid Caesar, for instance; Garry Moore; Peter Lind Hayes." Jack warmed to his subject.

"So he goes around with his toes sticking out of his shoes while others get rich on his material. I've said to him, 'Woody, why don't you get up and do this material yourself? Then you'll be rich and not the shlep that you are.'"

Woody lifted his eyes gravely at this buildup.

"The only thing you need is a showcase. You need The Blue Angel."

Jacobi and I weren't so sure. But Jack had brought us Harry Belafonte, and Mike and Elaine. Maybe he was right again.

"The salary isn't important," said Jack. "Pay him what you want. I want a place where he can stay awhile. I'll give you all the options you want. If he loses you any money, I'll pay his salary myself." Though Jack wasn't exactly broke, I took this as a metaphor.

So Woody opened at The Blue Angel.

Jack used to stand at the back every night, listening to Woody's show. During the intermission he'd walk Woody upstairs to one of the dressing rooms. I could hear Jack through the door. He'd call me in to add my voice to his.

"Tell him, tell Woody he's doing OK," Jack would beg. "He thinks he's terrible. He's ready to quit. You're doing terrific, do you hear? Terrific! Tell him."

Woody wasn't doing *that* terrific, a fact I didn't think it right to bring up at that particular moment. Woody hadn't yet learned how to deliver. Only sophisticates who were tired of being assaulted by nightclub comics welcomed his low-keyed schlemiel delivery. But he was learning. We kept him three months. We weren't paying him the kind of money that hurt.

"Did you see *Annie Hall*?" I asked Jim.

"Saw it twice."

"That's what I'm talking about. He's the same now as he was then."

"So like I was saying," said Jim, "think of the thousands, the millions his pictures are making today. And after all these years you're into jazz at the Vanguard. I think of all the singing and comedy acts you used to find, and here you are reduced to presenting jazz combos," mused Jim.

"What's the matter with jazz combos?"

"So if you're making a buck, OK!"

"I'm making a buck, sometimes even two."

How many Woody Allens are there, and teams like Mike and Elaine, and singers like Harry Belafonte? And comedians like Lenny Bruce? It was a good thing I moved into jazz at the Vanguard. I admit it was tough during the early sixties. Kids who listened to music were on a rock 'n' roll binge. And I didn't know my way around jazz. Then in the late sixties and early seventies things started to happen. I began to find jazz musicians, fledgling jazz musicians who were going places: Chick Corea, Herbie Hancock, Keith Jarrett, others.

"Kids were growing up and graduating from rock 'n' roll. They began to listen to jazz. Jazz musicians who had immigrated to Paris and Stockholm during the lean years returned to their native land and found audiences awaiting them. Jazz is big today," I informed Jim. "Haven't you heard?"

"All the men you gave jobs to when nobody else wanted them should remember that," said Jim.

"They do," I said. "Keith Jarrett, the piano player, did four nights at the Vanguard last year at seven hundred fifty a night because I gave him a job at a time when no one else would. And in January he sent me two tickets to his concert at the Metropolitan Opera House."

"Jazz at the Metropolitan Opera House?" Jim said, surprised. "D'you know what, they should take a week off, all these musicians, stay out of the Metropolitan Opera House, Carnegie Hall, and Madison Square Garden, and do a week free for you at the Vanguard."

"Jim, I got news for you. Jazz owes me nothing. Jazz did more for me than I ever did for jazz. It's kept me in business."

12 : Sonny's the Greatest

Yeah, I know all about Sonny Rollins. He's up in the big time now. I didn't go to his Carnegie Hall concert last year. I was surprised he showed up, that he didn't go off somewhere by himself that night—down to the walkway under the Williamsburg Bridge like he used to do, carrying his horn with him—and blow the night away, alone, and to hell with the mob at Carnegie Hall!

Sonny's into the big money now. I know about that too—that place on Bleecker Street, the Gate: a converted laundry, seats five hundred, and pays him fifteen hundred a night weekends, whenever they can find him.

There was a time when if you wanted to hear Sonny Rollins, you had to come to the Village Vanguard to hear him. He played the Vanguard four times a year, every year for ten years, once as a sideman with Miles Davis but mostly with a quartet of his own.

There's sharp disagreement among critics and jazz buffs about the playing prowess of some jazz musicians, but not about Sonny. He's the greatest—the greatest tenor saxophonist of his generation. Dexter Gordon, Billy Harper, Johnny Griffin, all great tenor men, but Sonny's the greatest of them all—no two ways about it.

Don't ask me why I never book Sonny anymore, why it's been years now since he worked at the Vanguard. It never was easy tying Sonny down to a specific date.

I remember one year I couldn't find him. I had his phone number on Willoughby Street in Brooklyn, where he lived, but every time I tried it, I got his wife or mother-in-law.

He's got to be home sometimes, I thought. I kept trying. One morning at three A.M., I let the phone ring five minutes, when lo and behold I heard the receiver lifted. "Yah!" It was Sonny's voice. Sonny never says "hello."

"Sonny!" I shouted. I was always afraid he didn't hear me.

"How're you doin'?" he asked matter-of-factly, as if he talked to me every day. "What's happenin'?"

"I got a week open in November," I kept shouting.

"Who's in the joint this week?" he wanted to know.

I told him.

"I'll be down tomorrow night," he said. "Just got back from India." Sonny was always just getting back from Japan, Denmark, or Poland; this time it was India.

"It was a year later when he showed up at the Vanguard—just walked in one night. It was Sonny all right, a tall, powerful, black man, with a bull neck, dressed in a flowing white caftan. His large round head was cleanshaven except for a cross-shaped outline of hair on top. "Something religious," the other cats whispered when they saw him.

I knew Sonny was weird, but I wasn't prepared for this vision in white from India. He stood around smiling, countering every question with a benign, tired voice. Sonny was always like that—only now he was more so.

"He's been playing his sax out there in a cave in India—alone, man."

"Who told you?" I asked Al Dailey, Sonny's favorite piano player.

"He told me."

"What was he doing out there in India?"

"Meditatin', man, meditatin'."

(Incidentally, Al Dailey is the only piano player Sonny never fired. That's a record because Sonny never hired a musician he didn't fire at least once, and often right in the middle of a number. He once fired Elvin Jones, probably jazz's greatest drummer.)

When I suggested a drink to him, Sonny smiled a refusal. He didn't touch the stuff anymore. His religion wouldn't let him. And about a gig, he was taking no gigs for the present. He was having his teeth fixed. God knows how long that was going to take. So I crossed Sonny off my list again, hoping for better luck next time.

About a year later, I heard through the jazz grapevine that

Sonny was hanging out at George Richard's loft on Greene Street, or is it Prince, and that he was dressed in a suit like you and me, letting his hair grow and playing like a sonofabitch. So I said to myself, "Maybe the bastard is ready to go to work. But what's he doing hanging out in George's place? He certainly can't be getting more money at George Richard's joint than I can pay him."

George ran weekend jazz in his Soho loft. Orange lights, pillows on the floor, broads trying to get picked up, that sort of shit. Unemployed jazz musicians jammed there for peanuts three or four nights a week. Whatthehell was Sonny doing there?

I called up Al Dailey. Al assured me that Sonny wouldn't play in a sink like George's place. "We use the place to rehearse, afternoons—that's all. Sonny wants to get his chops in order after all that work his dentist did on his mouth."

"Who's he using?" I asked.

"A white cat he found in California on trumpet. Paid his fare to New York. Sonny is crazy about him. The cat stinks." Al didn't sound happy.

Another week passed. Al dropped in and told me that Sonny talked about calling me—wanted to get back on the scene. "Hasn't he called you yet? In that case, call him. Here's his new number."

So I started calling that new number every day, twice, three times a day, for a month—no answer!

"Let it ring, man, let it ring—you know Sonny!" said Al.

It was the middle of the night and I dialed the number again. Three minutes, four minutes, five minutes pass; then I hear Sonny's breathy baritone. "Yah!"

"It's Max, Sonny." I'm shouting again.

"What's happenin', man?" he asks as usual.

"I'll give you the three grand—I got a date in April—a Tuesday opening. Al is here now. I'll make out the contracts, and he'll take 'em over to you. It's only a little after three. Sign 'em—I'll wait until Al gets back. OK? A quartet? A quintet? Bring in anything you want."

And that's how it happened that Sonny opened on a Tuesday in April, four years ago—the last time he played the Vanguard. Naturally the place was jammed. It was Sonny Rollins! Everybody was waiting to hear him. He'd been away too long. The critics and their girls came down, the chief executive officer of a record company, and Sonny's first wife, raising hell. But mostly it was the jazz community that had been missing him that crowded the place, some who'd only heard him on records, never in person, and a lot of young cats, graduates from rock, who had heard tell of Sonny and were glad to pay their money to hear him, because Sonny was the greatest.

The lights went down. Al Dailey was at the piano. Beaver Harris, drummer, and the bass player were in their places. Next, up came a blond cat hugging a trumpet—Sonny's newest discovery from California. Then in slow succession, four men carrying saxophones trekked their way to the bandstand.

"How many men are there in Sonny's quartet?" I asked.

That's how Sonny is. He'll pick up musicians on the way, invite them to sit in with him. I thought I knew all the active jazz musicians in the New York area. I recognized Eddie Daniels and Rocky Boyd, but the rest were strangers to me.

Finally Sonny appeared, in a floor-length white caftan (Holy Moses, Sonny is still a Moslem, I thought), his head bald, with only that cross of hair on top. The screaming and applause that greeted him was something.

Sonny seemed oblivious to the crowd. He gave the down beat, stated the theme on his horn, then cut out to let the other instruments take over. Every man took a turn soloing while Sonny stood quietly listening, the rhythm section maintaining a pulsing, insistent beat.

Now it was Sonny's turn. After a few flourishes on his horn, he launched into a honking, ecstatic solo.

The musicians on the bandstand stayed with him at first but soon dropped their weak, supportive sounds. They seemed stunned by what was coming out of Sonny's horn, the thrusts, the swoops, the soft lyrical descents, the roaring cries. He went on like that for an hour, with every chorus different. He started a number, then segued into another, then a third, then found his way back to the original tune—nothing repeated, nothing trite. Only Al Dailey's piano punctuated Sonny with tentative, searching chords.

If I were a jazz critic like Whitney Balliett of *The New Yorker* magazine or Nat Hentoff or Gary Giddins of *The Village Voice*, I could describe his playing like it should be described. I'll say one thing—he was terrific and playing like the Sonny of old.

At the intermission, in the kitchen where the musicians hang

out between sets, I noticed Beaver Harris, sweaty and exhausted, slumped into a chair. "Man, that Sonny's too much.
He's too much," he kept saying. "He kills me, man, he kills me."

That's how it was with musicians who played with Sonny. He
scared the hell out of them. They were in the big league playing
with him. It was a challenge to their musicianship, to their
improvisational skills.

The blond trumpet player, looking scared, stood around saying
nothing.

The half-hour intermission was over, the second set about to
begin. Down went the lights again and up came the blond
trumpet player, still scared; then the bassist; then Beaver Harris;
and finally Al Dailey. The four saxophone men didn't show up. I
guess they'd had it. They probably felt that Sonny's invitation to
them to sit in didn't reach into the second set.

Ten minutes passed. The men were in their places, ready to
start the second set, waiting for Sonny. Where was Sonny? I
went looking for him, in the kitchen, the men's room, on the
sidewalk out front, and in the back—no Sonny. He was nowhere
to be found.

"Whatthehell's happened to Sonny?" I whispered to Al Dailey
at the piano.

"Probably on his way back to India."

"That's not funny, Al. Where's the bastard? Where the hell'd
he go?"

And do you know what? Sonny never showed up for the second
set. He vanished. And I haven't seen him since.

I was about to lock up for the night. Al was there. He stayed
with me to the end. "What d'you think, Al?" I asked him. "What
really happened to Sonny?"

"It's that blond trumpet player," said Al. "Like I told you, he
sounded great in California but terrible in New York. Sonny
couldn't take him."

"Why didn't Sonny fire him?"

"Dunno."

"How can a trumpet player sound great in California and
terrible in New York?" I asked Al.

"It's the vibes, man, the vibes!"

"What vibes?"

"Coltrane, Miles, Coleman Hawkins, Bill Evans, Mingus, and
Sonny himself, cats who've played here and left their vibes here,

man! Know what I mean? The vibes! That's what I'm talking about. That blond cat didn't belong in this company. The vibes scared the hell out of him!"

"Al," I said, "if you hear from Sonny, tell him if he can play his horn in a cave in India, *alone,* he can play his horn here at the Vanguard *alone.* Tell him I'll give him the same bread I pay the quartet."

I understand Sonny clips an electronic gadget to his horn these days—a pickup that will give his horn a bigger sound so he can hear himself above the electrified instruments he likes to surround himself with now.

Sonny doesn't need it; he doesn't need any gadgets. He doesn't need any electricity, not Sonny. He needs his horn. Let him stand up there alone and pour it out. Mark my word, Sonny will throw that gadget away. Because Sonny's the greatest.

I haven't seen Sonny since that night. I still owe him a night's pay.

13 : Miles—A Portrait

What do you do on a Saturday night when the place is jammed and the star of your show walks off the bandstand in the middle of a set because his girlfriend is drunk in some uptown joint and phoning him to come and get her? Of all the jazz men who have worked at the Vanguard, Miles Davis was the toughest to handle.

Miles always liked to get one thousand dollars front money before he'd open. If I didn't have it, he might open, but after the first set on opening night, he'd come up to me and, scanning the crowd, whisper, "Don't forget the grand if you want me to come in tomorrow night." Miles's voice is like no other voice I've ever heard. A loud whisper through fog and haze you can barely hear. You can hear it once you get used to it. And I was used to it.

"And move that fuckin' spot out of my eyes. Or turn the goddamn thing off altogether. I'll work in the dark, if that's the way you wanna run your place."

But whatthehell, he was money in the bank.

Miles belongs to the cool school of jazz. He invented it. You go up and you play what you're gonna play. If the audience likes it, OK; if they don't like it, OK. Sure, you expect people to be quiet and listen, but if they don't, they don't. You play the same, quiet or no quiet.

Miles never asks an audience to be quiet, as I've heard some jazz musicians do. In fact he never talks to the audience, never says a word to them. I asked him once, "Why not announce a number? Why not take a bow at the end of a number? Why not announce the names of the men in your band, let people know that you're Miles Davis? They don't know you, never saw you before, some of them."

He looked at me with a puzzled, suspicious look, as if I were crazy. "I'm a musician, I ain't no comedian. I don't go shooting my mouth off like Rahsaan Roland Kirk. Don't get me wrong, I like Rahsaan. If you want a big mouth in your place, don't hire me. I don't smile, I don't bow. I turn my back. Why do you listen to people? The white man always wants you to smile, always wants the black man to bow. I don't smile, and I don't bow. OK? I'm here to play music. I'm a musician."

I knew enough after a speech like that to leave Miles alone, and I did, except once when I asked him to play for a girl singer who used to hang out at the Vanguard Sunday matinees. It was in the late fifties.

"She's great," I told him. "I heard her at a benefit."

"I don't play behind no girl singer. Ask Herbie (Herbie Hancock, the piano player in Miles's sextet); if he wants to play for her, it's OK with me."

When Miles heard the three numbers she did—and the applause, he said, "What's her name? Bring her in, if you want to, but hire a trio to play for her. I won't play behind no broad."

The girl singer was Barbra Streisand. I put her into The Blue Angel later.

The Vanguard doesn't run Sunday jazz matinees any longer. Miles didn't mind playing them, but some musicians hated it. They felt that playing six nights straight in one week was enough. Thelonious Monk put it to me this way: "Man, I ain't gonna work no seven nights a week—not me."

When people ask me why the Vanguard doesn't run Sunday matinees anymore, I tell them, ask Thelonious Monk.

Sunday jazz matinees were great while they lasted. Most important, they brought in the kids in the afternoon, who grew up later to become full-fledged Vanguard customers at night.

When Gary Giddins, the jazz critic, was fifteen, he used to spend the two-dollar allowance his father gave him to go to the Vanguard to hear Miles Davis on Sunday afternoon. He'd come early, get a front seat. Miles was one of his jazz heroes. One Sunday, Miles, walking off the bandstand at the end of the first set, stopped to rub out his cigarette in the ashtray on Gary's table. "Here, save it," he said to Gary. "Some day it's gonna be worth some money."

Miles didn't coddle his audiences, or his boss either. "You talk, 'Man, this, man that!'" he once growled at me. "Don't talk to me like a black man. You're a white man and don't forget it."

I was in his house on West Seventy-seventh Street. Miles, neat, immaculate, in a tailored suit, dark glasses, asked me, "Did you go up to see my tailor like I told you?"

"Who can afford three hundred for a suit?"

"You're too goddamn cheap."

"If I was making the kind of money I'm paying you, I'd get myself one." I was paying him thirty-five hundred a week.

Miles used to like to putter around in his all-electric open-faced kitchen after playing all night. That's when he was hungriest—at five in the morning. Once he pan-fried a three-inch filet mignon, put a second one on for me without even asking me did I want it, could I eat it. We were in his living room and I was watching him wash it down with a bottle of beer, when a blonde girl I'd seen him with at the Vanguard the night before came ambling sleepily down the stairs from the bedrooms, awakened by the kitchen noises he was making. She sat herself on a chair, yawning, saying nothing.

Miles barely recognized her presence.

"Do you like her?" he whispered to me. "Go upstairs with her if you're not gonna eat."

"Miles, you're a bastard."

"What, you don't like her?"

He invited me to see the changes and improvements made in his house since the last time I was there. He led me into the bathroom to demonstrate the outsized, square-shaped, whirlpool bath.

"Try it," he said. "Have yourself a bath in a real bathtub."

"When are you opening at the Vanguard?" I asked Miles once when he hadn't worked there for a year. "I got a week open in May."

"Tomorrow night," he said. Miles believed in straight, fast answers.

"How much?" I asked.

"Six thousand," he said.

"You know the Vanguard can't pay that kind of money," I replied.

"Get yourself a bigger place. I don't like nightclubs anyway. I don't want to work a nightclub anymore."

(That's Miles's way of turning down a gig—asking for an impossible amount of money.)

"What's the matter with nightclubs? You've worked in 'em all your life."

"They stink! I make more in one night on a college date than you pay me in a week. And I don't have to take all that shit!"

"What're you talking about?" I knew what he was talking about: the unemployed musicians and ex-musicians; the pundits; the reviewers, columnists, and salesmen promoting fly-by-night jazz mags; the writers of liner notes on album covers; the record collectors; the heavyweights from Harlem; college kids bearing cassette recorders; the gossips, punks, and freeloaders who hang out in rooms where jazz is played.

"You know what I mean, Maaax."

Miles draws out my name like that when he wants to make a point.

"I can't stand the whole fuckin' scene. The cats comin' around, the bullshit, the intermissions. I hate intermissions. And you looking sore because I ain't up on the bandstand. And the people! "Play 'Bye, Bye Blackbird!' Shit! I don't drink now. I work out in Stillman's Gym four hours a day. I used to have to come down every night. Down to your plantation. Now I come when I want to come. On a college concert I do two short sets and I'm through. I don't have to hang around, listen to a lot of bullshit!

"I was playing Birdland one week. We're out front during intermission, standing around minding our own business. Broadway was crowded. A convention or something. A cop comes over. 'Move over,' he says.

"Sure. It's me. I'm the one blocking the goddamn sidewalk. I don't move. 'Move!' the cop shouts. I don't move. He gets his club out. I don't move. Lets me have it on the head. I wipe the blood off my head, but I don't move. I don't move for no goddamn cop. I don't move for nobody.

"It's like I say, I've had it with nightclubs. At the intermission during a college concert the kids come up asking for autographs. That's about as tough as it gets. I can take it. No sweat."

"How're you getting along with Jack these days?" I asked Miles. Jack Whittemore had been his agent for ten years.

"I'm getting rid of him!" he said.

"What happened? After all these years?"

"I was in Paris last year," he began. "I needed a few albums, a cut of my latest record. Friends, critics, broads wanted one. So I called up Jack in New York. 'Call CBS,' I told him, ' and tell 'em to call Paris and have their wholesaler here deliver a dozen albums to me in my hotel.' So what d'you think Jack said to me? 'Who do you think you are, Frank Sinatra?'"

"I'm getting rid of the bastard. What's Sinatra got I haven't got?"

Jack Whittemore called me the next day.

"Miles called, said he saw you yesterday. By the way, how's Miles feeling these days? I haven't seen him in a month. He said something about a week in May, that you got a week in May open. Right?"

"Right."

"He sounded interested. Maybe I can get him to take it."

"How much money?" I asked.

"Forty-five hundred."

"I paid him thirty-five hundred the last time."

"Miles said forty-five."

"Thirty-five," I screamed.

"Make it forty and I'll talk to him."

"Talk to him. Talk to the bastard. And wrap it up, Jack."

"You got him for forty—OK?" was the first message on my answering box when I walked in the next day.

Nights when Miles wasn't playing at the Vanguard he'd bring his current girl to The Blue Angel and order Piper Heidseick champagne. One night I told the waiter to hand him the check. He tore it in two and sent the waiter back with this message: "Tell your boss I'll never pay a check here. Tell him he's been underpaying me at the Vanguard for years. I gotta get even somehow."

14 : Twenty Years with Charlie Mingus

The last time I saw Charlie Mingus was in July 1978 on the lawn behind the White House, where President Jimmy Carter was throwing a party to commemorate the twenty-fifth anniversary of the Newport Jazz Festival. Charlie was in a wheelchair, had been in a wheelchair for more than a year, suffering from the same debilitating disease that killed Lou Gehrig, the Yankee first baseman.

George Wein, the producer of the Newport Jazz Festival, introduced Charlie, "the world's greatest living jazz composer," he called him.

Charlie couldn't stand up to take a bow, but a thousand people rose to their feet to give him an ovation. Jimmy Carter walked over to his wheelchair to shake his hand. Charlie sat there, unable to speak, tears streaming down his face.

I remember when George Wein wouldn't hire Charlie for the Newport Jazz Festivals. George didn't think Charlie was good enough or big enough to play in his festivals. One year, 1962 I think it was, Charlie, who felt his band was good enough and big enough, mounted a jazz festival of his own, a rebel jazz festival right next door to George's in Newport, Rhode Island. He got Max Roach and a lot of other jazz musicians who were sore at George Wein, to join him. He scared the hell out of George.

I kept thinking, standing there on the White House lawn, how George Wein would be goddamn glad to have Charlie's band play in his next Newport Jazz Festival, if he could get him. But Charlie isn't going to play in any jazz festival anymore, or in any nightclubs or anywhere else.

He was sitting there in his wheelchair, dying. In fact it wasn't long after that White House barbecue that poor Charlie did die.

A month later Dannie Richmond, the drummer in Charlie's band, came down to see me, looking for a gig for Charlie's old band, now leaderless and unemployed.

"I guess I'm the leader now with Charlie gone," Dannie said. "I talked to Charlie when he was still alive and told him I was planning to go down to see you one day. 'You know the music,' he said, 'you played it with me for twenty years. And I know the men in the band got to work.'

"Charlie was living on the forty-third floor of a high-rise building on Tenth Avenue. His nurse lit him a cigar and he was puffing on it when he said it to me, 'If anybody can play my music, Dannie, you can play it.'

"'How 'bout my using Eddie Gomez on bass?' I asked him. The bass was Charlie's old instrument.

"'Eddie is great,' he said.

"'And I'm going to call the band "Dannie Richmond Plays Charlie Mingus Jazz Workshop Quintet" with Eddie Gomez on bass. That's what I'm gonna call the band. Is that OK?'

"'OK,' said Charlie. OK! He said, OK. What else could he say?

"So when's your first open date?" Dannie asked me.

We were sitting at my desk in the kitchen.

"Without Charlie up there, who's coming to the Vanguard to hear the band?" I asked him.

"Plenty," said Dannie. "The music'll be the same. The men in the band will be the same men who were with Charlie. With Eddie Gomez on bass, the music'll be as great as ever."

Maybe, but who knows Dannie Richmond?

I told Dannie he was no Charlie Mingus. "People came not only to hear Charlie but to see him in action. They'd sit and wait for him to throw one of his fits, stop the music cold, right in the middle of a number, rage and fume at his men because he heard something he didn't like. They'd sit fascinated.

"Do you remember the night he hit Jimmy Knepper, the trombone player, right in the stomach, right on the bandstand? Why'd he hit Jimmy like that?"

"Charlie wanted to hear the number we were playing the way he wrote it," explained Dannie.

Dannie, thin, tall, wearing a large head of hair, spoke in the even, quiet, courtly accents of a black man from the South.

"You're right," he said. "I'm no Charlie Mingus. I'm not going to knock no trombone player's teeth out for striking a wrong note. But there won't be any wrong notes. We're going to play the music the way he wrote it. Dig? God knows, I played it for twenty years.

"Sure Charlie was quick with his fists," Dannie said and laughed gently. "So what? He didn't always get away with it. D'you know Charlie was once in Duke Ellington's band? And the Duke fired him because he punched Juan Tizol, the saxophone player, on the bandstand. When he fired Charlie, the Duke is supposed to have said: 'Had I known you were going to get into a rumble like that on the bandstand, I'd have written an intro to it.'

"Charlie threw a lot of punches, and I've seen him take a few too," Dannie continued. "Sunny Murry laid one on him in the Five Spot one night. And the night the word got around that Oscar Pettiford knocked him cold in a Harlem joint, the cats in the band hearing the news didn't mind showing intense personal satisfaction, as if Oscar had evened the score for them."

"All right," I said to Dannie, "maybe the music will be the same, but the money I used to pay Charlie isn't going to be the same."

"I don't expect it to be the same," he said. "Give me a minimum guarantee, and if we do the business, sweeten it up a bit at the end of the run, right?"

I gave Dannie my hand, and we set the date for his opening.

This was a big moment for Dannie, a sideman becoming the leader of his own band. He sat there thinking about it—thinking about his twenty years with Mingus—twenty years! And now he was going on his own.

"I don't care what they say, I loved Charlie," he said. "He never threw a punch at me. Twenty years together in all kinds of weather! Now he's gone."

So we sat in the afternoon gloom of the Vanguard that hadn't yet opened for the night, talking about Charlie Mingus.

"I remember the first time you and Charlie played the Vanguard, in 1958," I said. "Jimmy Giuffre's trio was here, and Charlie came down to hear them. Jimmy, a tenor saxophonist and jazz innovator, was experimenting with what he called

Swamp Jazz. He was attracting a small, intense audience. Don't ask me what Swamp Jazz was. Jimmy wrote The Four Brothers a great number for the Woody Herman band, when Stan Getz was a member of that thundering herd, and gave up that kind of straightahead jazz to probe the mysteries of Swamp Jazz."

Jimmy was from Louisiana and distilled some pretty fancy musical notions out of the Louisiana swamps, which he was offering to the jazz avant-garde at the Village Vanguard in New York.

"After listening to Jimmy's Swamp Jazz for half an hour, Mingus said to me, 'Let me bring my band over next Sunday so you can hear some jazz.' Next Sunday Mingus and the quintet arrived. You were on drums," I reminded Dannie. "I introduced Mingus, and he looked at the small, dedicated Swamp Jazz audience down in front, snorted, gave the downbeat and let go with his first number. The volume, the intensity, the blistering attack of the music made me gasp. I'd never heard Mingus before.

"When the time came for the second set, Giuffre suggested we wait to allow the place to cool down before he resumed his own Swamp Jazz experimentations. I let Jimmy go the next week and hired Mingus. I never heard of Swamp Jazz again. Mingus wiped it out."

"No, Charlie couldn't stand Swamp Jazz," Dannie said. "He couldn't stand the free-style jazz the cats started experimenting with either. 'That's not jazz,' he said. 'You don't have to be a musician to play that crap. Dogs can play it.' Charlie read where some critics called it the sound of the future. 'It's got no future,' he said, 'because it's the kind of music that goes nowhere.'

"Man, he didn't like jazz critics either," said Dannie. "He didn't like jazz promoters, he didn't like jazz record producers or jazz executives of all kinds, and he didn't like jazz nightclub owners."

"No, maybe he didn't like me," I admitted. "Still, one night he walked over to where I was standing at the bar, picked the cigar I was smoking out of my fingers, took a puff and handed it back to me. 'I love you, you bastard.'"

Charlie was funny like that. He felt exploited. If he worked for you, you were exploiting him. The money you paid him was never enough. Maybe it wasn't.

"He once held a knife in front of me," I told Dannie. "So what? I knew he wasn't going to use it."

"What about? Money, I suppose," Dannie guessed.

"He needed a cash draw. I handed him a roll of bills. It wasn't the amount he asked for, so he threw the whole roll up in the air and grabbed a knife."

"I remember that," said Dannie. "I, like a good boy, bent down and started picking up the bills."

"And the night he tore the front door off its hinges," I said, "because the sign outside didn't have the words *Jazz Workshop* on it. 'And it's Charles, not Charlie,' he shouted down the steps. He wanted to be known as Charles Mingus, not Charlie Mingus. I didn't make that mistake again." Then I asked Dannie, "How'd you stand it—for twenty years?"

"It was the music he kept writing. I don't know a greater jazz ballad than 'Goodbye Porkpie Hat,' he wrote when Lester Young died. Do you?

"No, it wasn't always easy," he continued. "Charlie was a ladies' man. He was a handsome bastard before he got fat and weighed three hundred pounds. He'd take jobs as a male model when things got tough. I saw pictures of Charlie, half naked, with three half-naked broads beaming at him in some porno mag. He always had some dame around, running his errands. He married four of 'em, I think it was four. Some he supported, some supported him. Don't ask me how. In the early years, when we had to take gigs—any gig—for peanuts to keep going, it was always good to have a dame around who could bring in a few bucks.

"One night we were closing at The Black Hawk, a hotspot in the San Francisco Tenderloin. Charlie was talking to one of the girls who hung out in the joint. Her pimp came up, saw Charlie talking to his girl, didn't like what he saw, didn't want no goddamn musician poaching on his territory.

"Words passed. Charlie wasted no time. He swung a right. The pimp pulled a gun, fumbled it; Charlie kept swinging. The pimp went down, and Charlie stomped him till he lay quiet in the gutter.

"Charlie's foot swelled up so bad the next day I had to do all the driving all the way back to New York," Dannie said, shaking his head. "No, man, Charlie was no pimp. He was a ladies' man, like I said. It was good to have a broad around who could bring in a few bucks when things got tough. And Charlie had 'em. Dig?

"I watched Charlie step on a scale one day. We were about to board a plane for a gig in London. He weighed three hundred seven pounds. He didn't believe it. 'You can't eat a half-gallon of ice cream at every meal,' I told him. 'I've got to do something about it,' he said.

"Two weeks later, after we got back from London, Charlie went up to Dick Gregory's health farm; Dick, the ex-comedian, and his wife were running it somewhere in Massachusetts. Dick had a strict way of thinning you down: juice in the morning and one lean meal at night. That way you'd lose two pounds a day—guaranteed. In a month, sixty pounds.

"Charlie stood it for a week. Then he heard that Rahsaan Roland Kirk was playing at a place in Boston. So he told Dick he'd drive to town at night, hear Rahsaan, and be back in the morning. Right next to the place in Boston where Rahsaan was playing was a Chinese restaurant. Charlie saw it, hesitated a moment, and walked in. He didn't come out for a week. I mean he didn't get back to Dick's farm for a week." Dannie and I looked at each other for a moment before we started to laugh.

Then I asked Dannie, "What year was it that Charlie retired? Gave up playing jazz, swore he'd never play again? What year was that? '68, '69? That's when he holed himself up in his pad—a couple of furnished rooms on East Fifth Street—had his telephone disconnected, and refused to see anybody. He'd had it: the musicians, employed and unemployed, coming around bullshitting; the kind of joints he had to play in; the jazz buffs, sober and drunk. He was through with all that.

"Nobody saw Charlie for a year. Then I heard from a cat who ran into him one afternoon in a bar on First Avenue. The cat was a filmmaker, had moved to the Village to become a documentary filmmaker.

"'How did Charlie look?' I asked the filmmaker, and he said, 'Terrible.' And when he asked Charlie where he'd been for a year, what do you think Charlie did? He pulled a piece of paper out of his pocket, a dispossess notice his landlord handed him that morning, and said, 'That's where I've been.'

"So what do you think happened?" I asked Dannie. "This embryo filmmaker gets a bright idea. He says to Charlie: 'Go home, don't make a move. I'll be there in an hour.' So in an hour he's in Charlie's pad with a rented camera. And he starts shooting a documentary of Charlie getting dispossessed, an hour-long documentary of Charlie getting thrown out of his East Fifth Street pad.

"It's all there: the cops and Charlie's six-year-old daughter, Charlie's furniture on the sidewalk, his bass fiddle, his upright piano, his record player, sheets of music strewn all over the street. A city sanitation truck is loading it all 'to take it to a warehouse on Thirty-fourth Street,' the driver says on camera. There's a good shot of the landlord shouting at Charlie: 'Get outta here, you bum!' At the end a television reporter, his microphone stuck in Charlie's tearful face, wants to know 'What's up?'

"'Let people see what happens, what can happen to jazz in this bright land of ours,' says Charlie, or words to that effect."

"You were there," I said to Dannie. "I saw your face in some of the shots."

"Yeah, I sure was there."

"And two years later Charlie won a Guggenheim Fellowship. Fifteen grand!" I reminded Dannie.

"I was there when that happened too. Yessir! Did you ever read Charlie's book he started writing about that time, *Beneath the Underdog?*"

"No, I tried to read it but couldn't make it—because Charlie never wrote it."

"What do you mean, never wrote it? Who wrote it?"

"I know he didn't write it because I once read a manuscript Charlie wrote in longhand, about his early turbulent years in California. He showed it to me. It took me three hours to decipher it. When I got through reading it, I knew it was by Charlie. It was wild, angry and mean, like Charlie. I dipped into *Beneath the Underdog*. It's got Charlie's name on it, but it isn't Charlie. I know the girl who wrote it. Besides, why do I need to read a book about Charlie? I knew Charlie for twenty years. What I want to hear about Charlie is the music he wrote and played all his life."

I told Danny I had a good chance to hear some again the other night when I got home after closing the Vanguard. WKCR, the Columbia University Radio Station, was running a twenty-four–hour memorial marathon of Charlie's music. I turned on my radio, and the music came pouring out. One number after another—frenzied, heated, rhapsodic jazz music.

Charlie won't be playing those numbers anymore, I kept thinking, sitting alone at four in the morning, hearing the same ones he used to play at the Vanguard on and off for twenty years until I couldn't afford him anymore. "Better Git It in Your Soul," "Love Is a Dangerous Necessity," "Self-Portrait in 3 Colors," "Meditation in Times Square." What titles!

I asked Dannie about one of Charlie's numbers I'd almost forgotten: "All the Things You Could Be Now if Sigmund Freud's Wife Was Your Mother."

"Yeah!"

"Sounds like one of Charlie's love songs," I said.

"It is. Duke Ellington's 'All the Things You Are' inspired him to write it. Charlie loved the Duke. He wrote 'Open Letter to the Duke.' Did they play that one?"

"No, but they played 'Eat That Chicken.'"

"Charlie could be funny," said Dannie.

"I couldn't tear myself from that radio. It must've been six o'clock before I got to bed."

Dannie rose from his chair. Everything was agreed between us: the date, the money, and how the ad announcing his opening was to read:

Twenty years with Mingus, Dannie Richmond plays The Charlie Mingus Jazz Workshop Quintet with Eddie Gomez on bass.

My phone rang a couple weeks later. It was a woman's voice on the other end telling me she's the secretary of Mrs. Mingus.

"I've heard you're planning to book Dannie Richmond into the Village Vanguard using the Mingus name," she says. "If you do that, Mrs. Mingus expects twenty-five percent of the money you're paying Dannie to be held out, kept for her in escrow. Do you understand? Mrs. Mingus has a lawyer."

Then she hangs up.

When I told Dannie what had transpired on the telephone, he hung his head a moment. "That's Sue," he said. "I didn't know Charlie was married to her—or is he? Like I've been telling you, there's always some dame around, running Charlie's errands for him. And it looks to me like there still is."

Dannie opened at the Village Vanguard on February 6, 1979. Every night when he came to work the first thing he said to me was, "Sue was on the phone with me again today for an hour. She doesn't want to be left out. She wants me to help her stay with Charlie's music that she loves. Wants to bring back Charlie's men, wherever they are, put a band together and call it The Charlie Mingus Dynasty Band—with me on drums."

"With you as the leader, right?"

"No, man, she wants to be the leader."

"How can she be the leader?"

"That's what I keep telling her. 'Sue,' I tell her, 'I'm the leader. I've played Charlie's music for twenty years. You love the music, but *I've played it* for twenty years.'"

"Dannie," I advised him, "let Sue call herself the leader if that's what she wants. You know and every man in that band'll know you're the leader. Let her stay with Charlie's music. Give her something to do, sign papers, anything, and give her twenty-five percent."

He looked me straight in the eye and said, "When you book The Charlie Mingus Dynasty Band at the Vanguard, brother, if you want to give her twenty-five percent, you give her twenty-five percent. But out of your money, not mine. Dig?"

15 : Rahsaan Roland Kirk— In Memoriam

Rahsaan Roland Kirk, the jazz musician, died on December 5, 1977. He was forty-two years old.

"Like a lot of jazz musicians he died young, too young," said the Rev. John Gensell, the jazz pastor, at his funeral.

For fifteen years, three, sometimes four times a year, he played the tenor saxophone at the Vanguard with his quintet. Rahsaan also played an alto saxophone, a soprano saxophone, a baritone saxophone. He played a clarinet, a flute, and a trumpet he outfitted with a reed mouthpiece. Then he played a "stritch" and a "marzella," stumps of horns that never made it as saxophones. He found them in a Lower East Side pawnshop and liked the kind of sounds he could get out of them.

If you saw him in his black beret and dark glasses, pushing his cane in front of him through the crowded chairs and tables of the Vanguard, step up to the bar, find the kitchen, the men's room, the telephone on the wall, without anyone nudging or prompting him, you might wonder was he really blind? If you offered to help him, he'd turn you down politely. Customers asked me if he was born blind, and I had to admit I didn't know. I never asked him.

He'd come on the bandstand wearing three saxophones on his chest. People seeing him for the first time wondered what the hell was going on. Next to him on the bandstand was a "sound tree," on which he hung bells, gongs, whistles, a tambourine, chain clusters, and a small percussive drum he could reach as the music prompted him. One night he brought in a long flute he'd fashioned out of bamboo. It was for four players. He called up men out of his band to help him demonstrate it.

Rahsaan was never satisfied. If his flute wasn't coming across the way he wanted it, he'd add his voice to it—and the combination of voice and instrument was something to hear. He'd play two instruments at once, sometimes three—a reed section all by himself. Jazz music drove and consumed him.

Rahsaan liked the vibes at the Vanguard, liked them so much that he'd work there for less money than in places "where the vibes say nothing to me"—Avery Fisher Hall, Carnegie Hall. "I got nothing against money," he said. "I do college dates. That's where the money is. I like to do 'em. The kids are great; they ask a lot of questions: 'What kind of jazz you playing?' Like that. White kids like to put a ring around things. There's nothing wrong with it, if they really dig jazz.

"First I play for them; then I like to sit around and rap with 'em. I like to talk to 'em about the blues, tell them about Louis Armstrong and Bessie, that Fats Waller was no clown. I like to talk to 'em about Coltrane, the Duke, Thelonious, and McCoy Tyner; about Mingus, who gave me a job when I first got to New York from Columbus, Ohio, fifteen years ago. Get 'em to feel the joy, the meaning of jazz—black classical music.

"Some people think maybe I talk too much. I don't go for the cool school of jazz where a cat stands up and barely acknowledges the presence of the audience. I like to get down among the people, let 'em hear me, get at 'em through the music I play. Give me my tenor and let me take off, and I feel if you're listening, there can never be any differences, any misunderstanding between us. What's jazz? It's the truth, man, the truth. That's what jazz is.

"If I'd had my sax that day in Akron, Ohio, if it hadn't been packed away in its case, those F.B.I. men who came swarming down on me would've realized that I, Rahsaan, could never be a man plotting to hijack no plane. That's right! Don't laugh. Hijack a plane! That's what they arrested me for in Akron when I was about to board a plane for L.A. Look it up, it was in the papers.

"I had this sword, a ceremonial sword given to me as a gift, packed away in my knapsack. And a small tear gas gun I always carry on New York streets at five in the morning. I was on my way to a gig in L.A., and the F.B.I. figured that with all that hardware, I got to be plotting to hijack that plane—take it to the moon. They held me two days in Akron before they decided to let me go.

"Like I say, if I'd been able to lay my hands on my tenor sax, adjust the mouthpiece, and play a couple of choruses of 'Liza Jane' or 'Prelude to a Kiss,' or maybe Thelonious's 'Round Midnight,' even an FBI man would've seen that this blind, black musician ain't gonna hijack no aeroplane."

Rahsaan called the people who came to hear him "believers." One night a nonbeliever was in the audience. He didn't like the "caterwauling" he was hearing and didn't mind saying so. Rahsaan stopped everything and laid down his horn. He knew exactly where that unbeliever was sitting. Rahsaan made his way over to the man, grabbed him, and ordered him to leave. He didn't want a nonbeliever in the place.

Rahsaan could sing. He had no voice, but that didn't stop him. He'd prepare the audience. "Sidney Bechet's 'Make Me a Pallet on the Floor.' Sidney didn't have a pallet on the floor to lay his weary head on in this country, so he went off to Paris to find one. No, man, this country ain't always been good to her jazz musicians.

"Got no pills, got no pot, I'll get high on what I got," and he'd finish the song with an angry laugh. Then he'd pick up his clarinet and go into a fast chorus of "When the Saints Go Marching In"—walk off the bandstand right into the crowd scrambling before him, march down the aisle, wailing, the trombone player behind him, up the front steps, out into the street, and back down again.

When Rahsaan heard through the jazz grapevine that Eddie Harris had electrified his saxophone, he said, "Man, I don't like all the electricity the cats are introducing these days—electric pianos, amps, fender bass, synthesizers. I like jazz clean and straight ahead. I don't like to see it made too easy. I like jazz that sweats. Hell, if you pull the cord out of the socket, these bands are out of business.

"We were doing two weeks at Ronnie Scott's in London. One night there was a blackout. The band playing opposite us couldn't go on. They were through. We finished the night by candlelight."

Rahsaan liked to talk about the cunning and machinations of the record companies. "Joe Henderson was in New York last week. His label wanted him to cross over, cross over to where the money is—put more juice in his horn, hoke it up, get his drummer to put more boom in his drums, go commercial and start selling some records. But Joe ain't made up his mind," said Rahsaan.

"Herbie Hancock's last album sold four hundred thousand. He moved to California and bought a house with a swimming pool. So Herbie made it. But Freddie Hubbard can't sleep nights since he crossed over. Yeah, I heard Chick Corea pulls down ten grand a night since he crossed over. What good does it do him? He gives it all away. Yeah, man, gives it all away to the Scientologists. Haven't you heard? Chick's a Scientology freak. You don't know what's Scientology? Why it's a cult, man, a cult that sucks money," Rahsaan said, then laughed his characteristic laugh.

"And d'ya hear what happened to Ben Riley? Ben, who used to play drums behind Thelonious till Thelonious got sick and gave up playing the piano. Ben was putting together a quartet of his own, so he brought a kid down to rehearsals, a drummer from a disco joint, to teach him how to get the disco beat on his drums.

"Ben, who played drums with Thelonious—the greatest—was gonna learn to play drums all over again. So he could get himself some of that money, he was gonna learn to play disco, rock, fusion jazz. And this kid with pimples was gonna teach him.

"But you know what? Ben never made it. Couldn't get his drums to suck."

"You're knocking yourself out," his wife Dahrsaan used to say to Rahsaan. "Take it easy. You're forty-two years old." But he wouldn't stop. When he wasn't playing at the Vanguard, Rahsaan was playing in Miami, Chicago, San Francisco, Poland, Japan, at the Montreux Jazz Festival in Switzerland, in the South of France—lugging his horns on his shoulder. One day as he was getting out of bed, he suffered a massive stroke that paralyzed his right side and the fingers of his right hand. His left side and hand were not affected.

His chops, his tongue, responded to therapy. When I phoned him at the hospital, his voice sounded pretty much like his own voice. "What's happening? Who's playing at the club this week?" were his first questions.

"Betty Carter," I told him. "I'll bring you a cassette of the first set when I come over to see you."

Once Rahsaan was out of bed, he didn't waste any time. He packed his tenor sax and his wife drove him to the saxophone factory in New Jersey that had once made him a present of that saxophone. Companies do that—make presents to famous jazz musicians. If Rahsaan played it—their brand of saxophone—they figured other musicians would buy and play their brand of saxophone. Rahsaan wanted to know if they could reconstruct it for the fingers of his left hand.

It took him three months to teach himself to play it again, get the sound right, fingering the saxophone with only his left hand. At last he was satisfied, and he called me one afternoon. "I'm ready when you're ready," he announced.

Six months after he left the hospital, he opened at the Vanguard again. The word got around that Rahsaan was back and playing again. So his following of believers was out in full force waiting to hear him.

"How's he going to sound after what happened to him?" they asked.

One staunch believer whispered to me, "If you hadn't heard him before, you'd never know it's only his left hand he's using. Sounds better than I thought he would."

But after listening to him for a while, I turned his microphone up a little. Maybe that way he'd get a bit more strength, more clarity in his horn. He finished the opening number, stood a moment, and went into his second number without announcing it. Just went into it. I figured maybe he'd announce it at the end, address the audience like he always did, take charge, embrace the people, or taunt them if he didn't like the way they were listening. But he didn't say anything.

When he didn't talk to the people, I knew he wasn't feeling good. He was playing good, but not feeling good.

Rahsaan didn't use his clarinet or flute once in the set. He stuck to the tenor sax. And no more playing three horns together now, like in the old days. That didn't bother me. He always sounded best on the tenor anyway. But he didn't talk—that's what bothered me.

At the end of the set, he took the arm of one of his men, who helped him off the bandstand.

Rahsaan didn't finish out the week. The first time in fifteen years he didn't finish his week.

16 : "Jazz Didn't Do My Marriage Any Good"

Thelonious Monk's quartet was playing at the Vanguard one night in 1970. I was talking to the Baroness Nica de Koeningswarter in the kitchen, which is also my office and the Green Room. We could hear Monk's piano through the half-open door. The kitchen is the only place at the Vanguard where you can talk. If you talk at a table outside while the music is on, somebody will always shush you.

"Darling," the Baroness was saying to me, "you can thank me that Thelonious was on time tonight. If I hadn't driven him down, he'd still be on Sixty-fifth Street waving for a cab. Cabs won't stop for him. They're afraid of him, a big black man gesturing wildly for a cab on the corner."

The Baroness spoke with the soft cultivated accent of a high-born English lady. She is of middle height, middle-aged, and inclined to fat. I've known her for almost twenty years, and I knew she wasn't really looking for any thanks from me for driving Thelonious down. She had driven him down before, would do it again, probably the next night.

"I asked Nellie to come tonight," she continued. "But you know Nellie, always tired. (Nellie was Monk's wife.) You're a cool cat, Max, and I don't mind your asking me questions, only *don't* ask me about Bird. Besides, you know all about it. It was all over the papers. Of course the papers didn't tell everything—how desperately ill poor Bird was, for instance. He was sitting and listening to a Tommy Dorsey record, 'Just Friends' (Bird was crazy about Tommy Dorsey). Suddenly he started spitting blood, jumped up, screamed, and fell at my feet. I called the house

117

doctor. But the doctor of the fashionable Stanhope Hotel wouldn't come. He wouldn't attend a black man dying in a white woman's apartment.

"The headlines in the papers were awful: 'Charlie "Bird" Parker, Famous Jazz Man, Found Dead in Fifth Avenue Apartment.'

"It didn't do my marriage any good."

She opened her purse, rummaged through the contents, and finally came up with what she was looking for—a snapshot of herself taken when she was on a safari in Africa. She handed it to me. She was slim and beautiful then, standing next to a handsome man with a gun under his arm. "That was twenty-five years ago," she said, smiling.

The Baroness smiles a lot. She extracted a long cigarette holder from her purse and asked the kitchen man to be so kind as to order her a Brandy Alexander. "Be sure to tell Mike it's for me."

I have always felt, when talking to the Baroness, that I'd better mind my manners and my language.

"When did you first hear jazz?" I asked her. "There were no jazz joints in London."

"My brother was a pianist," she said as if that explained everything.

"Lord Rothschild a pianist? A jazz pianist?"

"No, dear, he was a gifted amateur who played the piano at home. Bach, Beethoven, you know.

"But Benny Goodman used to bring his band to London for concerts in those days back in the forties. We'd go. Once my brother got the notion he'd like to take some piano lessons from Teddy Wilson. Teddy was Benny Goodman's pianist. That's when I first started to hear and listen to jazz.

"Teddy was charming. He'd let me sit and listen to the lessons. Afterward he'd play for me. He brought me some records, and I learned about a shop in London where I could buy some more.

"I discovered Duke Ellington's 'Black, Beige and Brown.' If you should ask me what record really converted me to jazz, I would have to say it was that one. I didn't know jazz could be so beautiful.

"When we first arrived in New York, we moved into the Stanhope Hotel across the street from the Metropolitan Museum. My husband was in the French diplomatic service and hated jazz. I, of course, looked up Teddy Wilson when we got here.

"New York was wonderful in those days: The Bird at Birdland, the Hawk at the Famous Door, Stuff Smith at the Onyx, Miles at the Vanguard, Thelonious at Minton's on 116th Street. I was out every night till five in the morning, sometimes with Teddy, sometimes by myself. I'd drive my Bentley everywhere and anywhere, nobody bothered me. I was excited, enchanted, sent by the music. I was hearing live all the men I used to hear on records in London. The first time I heard Thelonious play 'Round Midnight,' I cried.

"Of course jazz didn't do my marriage any good."

She paused briefly, then struck a different note. "I discovered something about jazz musicians. They were always unemployed. I couldn't understand it. Why should these wonderful, creative artists be chronically unemployed? Why should they be in such constant, grinding need?

"I thought I could help them." The Baroness smiled at the thought.

"I even became a manager. I undertook the job of managing a jazz band, believe it or not. Art Blakey and the Jazz Messengers, imagine! I thought I could help him and his men become more employable. Me! A manager! It was a disaster.

"I invested in six matching, blue tuxedos. I thought that would help get them jobs. I was out of my mind."

The Baroness seemed embarrassed by this revelation of her managerial incompetence. Perhaps she was telling more than she had bargained for when she agreed to talk to me about herself and jazz.

"One thing I shall never forget about America . . . I'll never forget the state of Delaware! I never knew it was below the Mason-Dixon line. That's what you call it in history books, the Mason-Dixon line, don't you?

"Thelonious had a gig in Baltimore. I promised to drive him there. At the last moment Nellie decided she couldn't make it. So here I was driving Thelonious and Charlie Rouse, his tenor man, through the state of Delaware on the way to Baltimore.

"I'll always remember Newcastle. It was blistering hot, and Thelonious was having one of his bad days—silent, sweating, and miserable. Finally he spoke up. 'Could we stop somewhere for a cold drink, a beer, a glass of water, anything?'

"I saw this sign, *Motel and Bar,* and stopped the car. As Thelonious walked towards the entrance, it occurred to me that maybe I should have gone with him. When ten minutes passed, I began getting nervous. As I got out of the car to find out what happened, a jeep drove up, ground to a halt, and two cops dashed up the steps. In a minute they came out with Thelonious between them.

"'Who are you?' one cop said, looking at me. I guess we did look pretty suspicious, two black men and a white woman in a foreign car. 'And who is this man? He won't give me his name. He won't talk.'

"'He's a musician,' I said. The cop ordered Charlie out of the car and frisked him. Then he rummaged through my purse and found a few strands of weed at the bottom, enough for one stick.

"Now the cops were sure they had the evidence for an arrest. We were addicts, criminals, and I was the pusher. They ordered Thelonious into their jeep.

"But Thelonious was so mad he wouldn't move. He took hold of the car door, darling, and couldn't be budged until one cop started beating on his hands with a billy club, his pianist's hands.

"I screamed as a crowd gathered.

"Well, they finally got us to police headquarters several miles down the road. Charlie and Thelonious were dismissed, but I had to stand trial. I was a dangerous criminal because of that bit of marijuana in my purse. I was found guilty and sentenced, mind you, to three years. Three years! And my Bentley was to be confiscated.

"My lawyer appealed, of course. I hired Edward Bennett Williams, and after almost two years of filing legal papers, conferences, probationary reports, letters from my brother and from the agent Joe Glaser, and from Nat Hentoff, the judge concluded I wasn't an addict or a pusher and dismissed me. It cost me a fortune.

"Needless to say Thelonious never made that gig in Baltimore.

"Darling, I never dreamed that Delaware could be such a mean, uptight little state. But the Du Ponts, had they wanted to, could have prevented the whole sorry mess with no trouble at all. The Du Ponts have known the Rothschilds for generations. But would the Du Ponts lift a finger? No, of course not." The Baroness wasn't smiling now.

"I know people think I'm pretty weird, Max. They can't understand my interest in jazz and my friendships with jazz musicians. They think it's something sexual, something obscene.

"Take the Hawk, for instance. Do you remember the night he took a fall on your bandstand? Then when the ambulance came and the doctor wanted to take him to St. Vincent's, he wouldn't go. Instead, after resting a half-hour, he had a chair brought up to center stage, and finished the set sitting down.

"I ran across the street to get him a container of soup. The Hawk would never eat. I'd drop into his place, open his refrigerator—nothing. I'd bring him a bottle of milk, some fruit, some egg rolls—he was crazy about Chinese food.

"You didn't know it and I don't think you know it to this day, but Coleman Hawkins was epileptic. In his apartment on Central Park West, where he lived alone, I had several telephone extensions installed. One phone was on the floor, so if he ever took a fall when he was alone he could somehow reach it and call for help.

"I loved the Hawk, we were friends. The poor bastard had to go and die." A burst of applause sounded from the crowd listening to Monk and his quartet and brought the Baroness back to the present.

"You know, Max, Thelonious used to come over to the house often and play for me. When he wasn't playing the piano, he loved to play Ping-Pong. I had a Ping-Pong table put on the porch. He was the swiftest Ping-Pong player I've ever known; he was uncanny. Now that he's not feeling so well, he doesn't play the piano as much as he used to, or Ping-Pong either. I'm thinking of getting one of those small pool tables. I wonder, are they expensive?

"You dig me, that's why I'm telling you this," she told me. "I think you dig me because you're cool, Max; you're a cool cat. The Hawk used to say that about you."

"Nica, what's happened to his horn? I'd like to get a hold of it, put it under glass, and hang it on the wall next to the bar."

"You're mad," she said smiling. "Maybe I do come from a weird *mishpocho,* but we're a close family, Max, believe it or not.

I'm often in London and my brother is often in New York. Last year my sister, Miriam, on her way home from Australia, stopped off in New York to see me. She had spent a year in Australia researching fleas, that's her bag. And both my daughters live with me. They all forgive me my interest in jazz."

17 : The Last Speak-out, or How the Vanguard Almost Got Busted

I didn't recognize him right off, but there he was in full color on the cover of *The New York Times Sunday Magazine*—Baba Ram Dass, the guru, in a long beard and flowing white robe. Inside was the story of his rise and fall and rise. Baba Ram Dass he calls himself now, and he's a guru, by God.

I remember him fourteen years ago at the Vanguard, when he was plain Dick Alpert. He was clean shaven then, wore glasses and a business suit, and his hair was always combed as neatly as an aspiring junior executive's.

Back then, instead of closing the Vanguard Monday nights as we'd done for years, I installed the Speak-Out, a free-for-all devised by me and Paul Krassner, publisher and editor of *The Realist*, a small radical rag, published now and then when Paul had the money to pay his printer.

A speak-out was just what it said it was: a time to speak out on the controversial subjects of the day—What's Wrong with Prurience? Is Satire Futile? Atheism: The Fifth Freedom; Civil Disobedience and the Law—subjects like that. Paul Krassner and I enlisted a panel of four every Monday night to speak out. The panelists included Nat Hentoff; Ralph Ginsberg, publisher of *Eros;* Barney Rosset of Grove Press; Percy Sutton, before he became Manhattan Borough President; John Simon the critic; the Rev. Howard Moody; Mario Savio, the leader of Berkeley's Free Speech movement; Richard Kuh, who later prosecuted Lenny Bruce; and Harvey Matusow, the reformed F.B.I. rat, among many others. Norman Mailer told me he wouldn't go on a panel for the "ridiculous twenty-five bucks" that was the going fee.

Feeling ran high on Monday nights. After the panelists spoke out, the audience spoke out, asked questions. Audiences paid three bucks, the price of admission, often for the privilege of being savaged by a panelist or a heckler. Paul kept reasonable order with a big cowbell.

One Monday night, before he changed his name to Baraka and moved to Newark, the poet Le Roi Jones hurled insult after insult at the predominantly white audience. Even Paul, with his cowbell, gave up. I had to close early that night.

After about six months, the Speak-outs began to lose steam, and with one scheduled Speak-out to go, I decided the hell with them. As things turned out, this last Speak-out was the wildest of them all. It could have been the last of the Vanguard too.

I had first heard of Alpert when he and Tim Leary were kicked out of Harvard. They were research psychologists running something they called the Laboratory of Human Development on the campus. Here they conducted experiments on the human psyche, feeding LSD to undergraduates to see what would happen to them. "What will LSD do to a person's brain—his thirteen billion–celled computer?" they asked. (For the squares: LSD is lysergic acid diethylamide, a hallucinogen, or mind-boggling, drug.)

A couple of Leary's and Alpert's students, you may recall, landed in mental institutions. So Harvard decided to throw Dick and Tim out and put their Laboratory of Human Development out of business. All this made headlines in the Village joints, hangouts of the literati and cognoscenti, where LSD was enjoying a vogue among young and not-so-young people looking for bright new horizons.

At about the same time, the federal government stepped in and, declaring LSD dangerous, forbade its use. "Tune In, Turn On, Drop Out"—the LSD theme song enunciated by Dick and Tim—made the government nervous. The government didn't want radical middleclass kids to "drop out," go off on shoplifting binges, or place bombs in banks and public buildings, like some were doing.

Dick and Tim believed in LSD, and in their Laboratory of Human Development. "You got to go out of your mind to use your head," they said. They believed that properly ingested, under the supervision of a doctor or a guru, this drug could work wonders on the human mind, stretch and expand it, open it up to new and unheard of awareness and consciousness, make a man so smart in fact, that nothing could ever fool him again—nothing that the government could ever say or do, for instance. That's why the government made LSD illegal, said Dick. The government was afraid it'd be found out if voters started illuminating themselves with LSD.

The only thing needed was a place to carry on the research that Harvard had interrupted. The government ban on LSD was a problem, though Dick and Tim felt that the government would eventually repeal its ban on this wonder drug. Meanwhile there were other ways, other researches into the mind of man that could be pursued, to hear them tell it.

There was controlled movement for instance, exercise, jogging, dance; diet and meditation; psychodrama; there was color and lighting—the strobe light, for instance, which can start you hallucinating. There was deep breathing. Stand in front of a window for a half-hour and breathe deeply first in one nostril then the other and see what happens. Can zonk you out. And then there was sound—music—jazz music. All these research strategies scientifically administered could do wonders to your psyche, Dick and Tim believed. "They'll have to do until the government repeals its ban on LSD, which we're working on," said Dick.

So Dick and Tim set up their laboratory in a sixty-five–room house on a four hundred-acre estate near Milbrook, New York, owned by a hip lady, Peggy Hitchcock, who believed in them and in LSD. Peggy believed in them so much that, although it was rumored some of her neighbors complained that land values of their estates were being hurt by the traffic generated by Dick and Tim's research lab, especially on weekends, she wouldn't think of evicting them.

"Why don't you take a weekend off and drive up to Milbrook?" the Baron Bjorn von Schlebrugge asked me one night.

The Baron was a Swedish baron, a stooped six-footer, with a long face and blond hair down over his ears. He was a dedicated jazz buff, had heard of the Vanguard in Stockholm, and decided he'd have to come to New York and see the place for himself. The night he arrived at Kennedy Airport he took a cab straight to the Vanguard, not even bothering to call up the friend on West Tenth Street, where he was going to stay while in America.

Once here the Baron started hanging out at the Vanguard. He was there every night, never missed one. This went on for months. Then one Friday night a waiter noticed that the Baron wasn't at his old station at the bar. What'n hell had happened to the Baron? But on Tuesday he was back "digging the sounds" like always.

Along about this time the Baron's mother, a graying aristocratic old lady, arrived at the Vanguard to see what had happened to her son in America—and to bring him back home to Sweden if she could. But the Baron wasn't ready to go home.

"The Baron's sure starting to get around," one waiter said. "He's got a new schedule; weekdays at the Vanguard and weekends in Peggy Hitchcock's house in Millbrook, where Dick Alpert and Tim Leary have set up their Laboratory for Human Development."

"You'll hear some great jazz up there," said the Baron, pressing his invitation. "Great, man! You know all the cats. They've played for you at the Vanguard, man. They sound better up there. The place jumps. Tamara dances—you know Tamara— a beautiful chick. She dances in the show Dick's put together. So why don't you take a weekend off? Dick'll love to see you. Tim is in India with his guru, but he'll be back. It'll do you good, man."

"I'm no LSD freak," I told the Baron.

"Hey man! They're not handing out that shit up there. No LSD—LSD's illegal. Didn't you hear?" The Baron smiled. "Know what I mean? It's illegal, man! There're other ways to open up your head. You gotta hear Dick tell it like it is. Dick gives a lecture after the show—the Psychedelic Show, man. That's what Dick calls it. I run the lights. It jumps, man!" (Though the Baron had been in America less than a year, he was already talking like the black jazz musicians he hung out with.)

Like I said, I was still looking for an idea for Monday nights, and in any event, for the final Speak-out. So I said to the Baron, "Why don't you ask Dick if he'll bring his psychedelic show right down here? He can rent a truck. I'll pay for it. And you can all pack everything—cameras, strobe lights, projectors, turntables, cables, all your hardware—and bring it down to the Vanguard.

Dick will star in the show. Tamara will dance; you, Baron, will run the lights; I'll supply the jazz band. We'll charge a four-dollar admission. And I'll contribute two hundred bucks to Dick's Laboratory of Human Development."

"Perfect, man," exclaimed the Baron.

The Baron didn't waste any time. He appeared the following Tuesday after his weekend in Millbrook, excited and glowing with news. "Dick is crazy about the idea. It'll be a first, the first time the Psychedelic Show will be shown in public anywhere! A great opportunity to spread the word in defense of LSD."

How to present the show to the public? I worked out the presentation plans with the Baron and he took them back to Millbrook for Dick's approval. I got out an ad and some publicity with this message: "If you swallowed a capsule of LSD, which you didn't, because LSD is illegal (the government says so), here's what would happen to you if you did. The Psychedelic Theatre in its first public appearance will show you: A Night of Simulated LSD Experience."

Once the date was set, the word got around, and that Monday night the Vanguard with its one hundred twenty-three seats was jammed with three hundred people. Outside, hundreds more were milling about trying to get in.

I saw only rare glimpses of the show. I was too busy watching the door and helping the cashier disabuse people who expected a piece of LSD with the price of admission. Whenever I could, in the darkness, I'd check the Baron, who was in charge of the 16mm movie camera and light projectors.

The show began. The Baron struck a Japanese gong and threw a white spot on the stage revealing a young man in a black leotard, handsome, bare-chested, grim-eyed. A bass fiddle was heard in the darkness. "That's Steve Swallow," whispered the Baron. "He doesn't look like Steve to me," I whispered back. "I mean the guy on the bass fiddle," said he. "You can't see him— used to play with Stan Getz."

For ten minutes the handsome fellow in the leotard gave an eye-filling demonstration of yoga and deep breathing while Steve kept bowing his bass fiddle. It *felt* like ten minutes.

Blackout!—and the Baron hit the Japanese gong again. Then a lighted candle, a guy holding it. I heard a priestly voice in the darkness intoning a prayer or maybe a manifesto.

There're no introductions in this show, I thought to myself, no warnings, no notion of what's coming next. There goes the Japanese gong again.

The movie camera started chattering. On the screen appeared a frog, the embryo of a frog being born. It took ten minutes for the frog to make it. "Life emerging," intoned the priestly voice. A saxophone accompanied life emerging, then blackout.

The screen lit up again. This time it showed flowers in color, moving. The saxophone was teasing the flowers. A red balloon appeared. It was falling, careening helplessly in the wind. The saxophone was teasing the balloon.

Blackout, and the Baron struck the Japanese gong again. I heard a roll on the snare drums in the darkness, then a mighty boom on the bass drum, and suddenly a strobe light began to blink on the stage, then another strobe light. Tamara, in a bikini, was inside the pulsing, throbbing spastic light, belly-dancing. The drums were urging her on. She was indeed as beautiful as the Baron had said.

Blackout and all the house lights went on.

Dick Alpert, looking like an overage graduate student, came out smiling and happy. He was met by prolonged applause and screams of welcome. He wanted to say a few words and answer some questions. He was happy to see the outpouring of people. He was happy to find the interest and support shown him.

Tamara, dressed in a sari and carrying a tray, began passing out jelly beans. There was a feeling of happiness and celebration.

"Are there any questions?" asked Dick.

A lady raised her hand. "Why has the government made LSD illegal?" she wanted to know.

"Because the government is afraid, that's why," he said.

There were other questions and answers, but this was the theme of the night—the government ban on LSD. Someday soon, Dick said, he hoped that this beneficent drug would be made available to mankind again.

It was 5 A.M. by the time we cleared everyone out of the place. It wasn't easy. Then we sat down to assess the night: the Baron; Ralph Metzer and Richard Hollingsworth, aides and followers of Dick's; Pete La Rocca, the drummer; and Steve Swallow, the bassist. We agreed, it was a great night.

"I didn't know Dick had such a big following," I said. "But what was the constant commotion near the door all about?"

"Oh, people going out for a bit of fresh air and making sure the cashier will let them get back in again," said Pete casually.

"What was outside beside the fresh air of Seventh Avenue?" I asked.

"Plenty," said the Baron smiling.

"What d'you mean, plenty?" I asked again.

"Plenty."

"I didn't see any deals, any sales, any money passing," I said. "I didn't see any LSD."

"What does LSD look like?" asked the Baron still smiling.

"I don't know. I've never seen any," I had to admit.

"It wasn't Tamara's jelly beans," said Pete. "But half the crowd was high."

"High? Half of 'em were high?" I repeated blankly.

"That's what Pete says." The Baron gave me a patronizing smile. "Somebody was handing the shit around, man."

"Who was handing what shit around?" I almost screamed.

"Take it easy, man," said the Baron. "I never saw a bigger crowd in your joint. You could run the Psychedelic Theatre *every* Monday night—make a fortune."

"Every Monday night!"

"Yeah, man, why not? Nothing happened. Tim Leary'll be back this week and I'll talk to him."

"Nothing happened? You say nothing happened? I could've lost my goddam license, that's what *could've* happened."

I thought I could spot anything and everything at the Vanguard. And God knows I have in all the years I've been in the nightclub business: cops, drunks, neighborhood guerrillas looking for a fight, guys walking out on checks, stags bothering women, a female celebrant perched on a table dropping her skirt for all to see. I could spot and handle them all.

I didn't know I could be taken for a square by a Swedish baron and a bunch of psychedelics from upstate New York.

18 : The Russians Are Beautiful Cats

One afternoon a State Department aide called me from Washington, D.C. and asked me: Would the Village Vanguard favor sending the Thad Jones–Mel Lewis Band to Russia?—this steaming, swinging jazz band of seventeen men that was playing at the Vanguard every Monday night with an occasional week thrown in and that had been playing at the Vanguard for eight years of Monday nights, in fact. Would I favor sending them to Russia to bring jazz to the Russians? The Russians would send us a company of ballet dancers or a stage full of Siberian folk singers in exchange.

"Fantastic!" proclaimed Thad and Mel, the leaders of the band, when I told them what the State Department had in mind.

"This time you gotta come along with us, Max," said Thad. "You didn't make it with the Band to Japan last year. Besides, you come from Russia, don't you?"

"Yeah! My mother brought me from Vilna in the steerage with the baggage when I was maybe two years old."

"Then it's settled," said Thad.

The State Department figured the Vanguard Band would make fine good-will ambassadors in the cultural exchange program then going on with the Russians. Thad was black; Mel was white and Jewish; Dee Dee Bridgewater, our vocalist, was black and beautiful; Jerry Dodgion, the alto saxophonist, was white; Richard Davis, the bassist, black. Like that. A band of seventeen white and black musicians playing jazz, and playing it together, at the Vanguard.

A State Department escort assigned to the Band met us in London. He looked like a graduate student, spoke Russian, and

130

his name was Bob. We got on first-name footing with him immediately. Thad could do that—Thad, two hundred pounds, six foot four, broad-faced, beaming, happy and full of juice.

When the Band landed in Leningrad, we found twenty Russians at the station waiting to greet us. (Russian jazz musicians we later learned.) They were waving and smiling from behind a picket fence manned by two Russian cops. One of them kept flashing an old picture of Thad when he was with the Count Basie Band. We walked over to them. Miracle of miracles, they spoke English! We could understand them!

One Russian recognized Jimmy Knepper, our trombonist, remembered him when Jimmy was in Russia with the Benny Goodman Band ten years ago. Another Russian hailed Dee Dee Bridgewater. He had met her last year when she was in Russia with the University of Illinois Jazz Band.

Who was I? one Russian wanted to know. I didn't look like I belonged to the band.

"He's the impresario of the Village Vanguard!" cried Thad, punching my shoulder. Thad liked to thicken things up a bit.

"The Village Vanguard!" They knew all about the Village Vanguard. "Sonny Rollins, Live at the Village Vanguard! John Coltrane, Live at the Village Vanguard!"

They had the records in their collections. And Dizzy Gillespie's "Blues for Max"—they had that record too. "So, that's Max! Max Roach!"

"No, comrade, that's not Max Roach. That's another Max," said Thad.

"These Russian cats are beautiful," he whispered to me.

Thad had brought along a carton of records the Band recorded "Live at the Vanguard."

If they'd drop around to the Moskva Hotel, he told them, where the Band was to be billeted, he'd be glad to pass a few around. And to be sure to come backstage after the concert tonight, the first of five concerts the Band was scheduled to give in Leningrad.

We discovered on our arrival that the demand for tickets had been so great that the Russians had to move the site for the concerts from their October Hall with three thousand seats to a converted ice hockey rink seating six thousand.

The lobby was full when we got to the hotel. One Russian brought his girl, a singer, to meet Thad. She had flown in from

Tbilisi for the concert that day, wore a red pants suit, like our girls at home, and spoke English. She had a band of her own in Tbilisi it turned out, and had "one jazz number in her repertoire," she proclaimed proudly.

Our band was to give a concert in Tbilisi later on in our tour, but she was scheduled to be in Turkey with her own band at that time, so she flew one thousand miles to Leningrad to hear us. She said she wouldn't miss our Band for all the rubles in the world. "You don't often get a chance to hear live jazz in Russia," she said.

"Beautiful!" cried Thad.

Russians in the lobby walked over and introduced themselves. One was a handsome bearded gentleman from Moscow, a physicist, who'd arrived in Leningrad that morning from Prague, where he had attended a concert of Dizzy Gillespie's Jazz Giants touring central Europe. Then, two brothers from Vilna, radio technologists, and a kid from Riga who had his visa for Israel, he told me later. They'd all come to Leningrad for the concerts, had bought tickets months ago.

Thad beamed at them. Would Cass, our baggage coordinator, if you please, run upstairs and bring down that box of records Thad had brought from New York? Thad broke open the box and pushed a record each on the Russians. You'd think he was handing them platters of gold, the way they received them. They couldn't believe their eyes, jazz records, precious jazz records.

Thad told them to forget it, that the Band, "the greatest Band in the land," had finished cutting a record just before embarking for Russia. He's got to get down to the business of mixing it once he gets back to the States.

"And I'll send you one when it's finished, if you'll just put your address down on a piece of paper."

One Russian confided to Thad that if he wanted to make sure they'd get the record, he should include a piece of printed matter of an educational nature in the envelope. Then the records would be delivered to them. Otherwise, a simple jazz record from the West might get lost in transit, know what I mean?

After some drinks at the small, stand-up bar on the terrace, Bob, the State Department man, reminded Thad that he better tear himself away from the Russians because dinner was about to be served in the upstairs dining room reserved for the Band.

"Could the girl singer from Tbilisi join the Band for dinner?" asked Thad.

"Hell no!" Bob said and reminded Thad that he wasn't at home, but in Russia, and not to forget it. "You can't invite a Russian to dinner in Russia."

Bob asked Cass could he please get the men moving in the direction of the dining room.

"*Payakile!*" cried Cass. He had just learned the word from one of the Russians and thought he'd try it out on us. "*Payakile!*" he cried again. "Let's get rolling, men!" he translated.

The Russians stood around smiling as they watched us heading for the stairs leading to the dining room.

What do you do in Russia after the concert on opening night? We gathered in Thad's room on the third floor, a large room, to celebrate and talk over what happened. "Would some of the Russian musicians and the girl from Tbilisi drop in to help us celebrate?" Thad had invited them.

Thad produced a bottle of vodka he had bought in the gift shop in the hotel lobby. "That's where you buy vodka in Russia, man—in a gift shop."

"D'you know the Russians invented vodka?" he asked, Roland Hanna, our piano player. "You've been drinking it all your life and you think it comes from New Jersey."

"And caviar! Did you know the Russians invented caviar? I dig the Russians. And the way they applaud? Together, in unison, like somebody up there leading 'em.

"They loved Dee Dee's singing. When she laid those Russian words on them that Bob taught her, that she was glad to be in Russia, man, those Russians went wild!"

Thad walked over to Dee Dee, took her head gently in his large hands, and planted a kiss on her forehead.

"Have some sugar, beautiful."

Then turning to me: "Why was the floor of the ice rink unused for seating?" Thad asked. "Why was only the grandstand seats surrounding the floor used, when there were so many people outside trying to get in? Must be a law," he guessed.

"At the Vanguard on Monday nights when the joint is jumping, law or no law, you'd sell the seat in the men's room. I've seen you do it," he cried, punching my shoulder and emitting a laugh that shook the room.

Thad soon discovered that everything happens early in Russia. It was only midnight, the Russians weren't coming, and the vodka bottle was dry. Thad asked one of the men to run down to the lobby for another bottle. The man came back empty-handed. The gift shop was closed. The lobby was dark, and the middle-aged lady guardian on the floor looked worried about the noise coming from Thad's room.

Thad was saying he could still hear the sustained applause of the six thousand Russians who packed that ice rink. And there were four more concerts scheduled for Leningrad! "Tomorrow night after the second concert," he said, "we gotta do something different.

"A Jam Session! That's it—a jam session with the Russian musicians, right after the concert tomorrow night. Right here in this room. There's plenty of room. Everybody'll bring his instruments, the Russians will bring theirs. We'll get a couple of bottles of vodka, some caviar. Did you bring any extra bread with you?" he asked me.

When Thad proposed the idea of a jam session to Bob who was with us, Bob looked worried. "That'll take some heavy negotiating with the Russians. The Department of Cultural Affairs. They've never heard of a jam session, and they're not going to like it."

Breakfast was at eleven A.M. in the small upstairs dining room assigned to the band. It was noon when Bob and his counterpart from the Russian Department of Cultural Affairs arrived. A large, thick-faced, curly-haired Russian—"Cannonball," Thad nick-named him, because he looked like Cannonball Adderly, the great alto saxophonist back home. They were late for breakfast because they'd been on the phone all morning, trying to reach the right man upstairs in the Russian Cultural Affairs offices who could say, "da" or "nyet" to the jam session idea that Thad had proposed.

They'd finally reached him. A decision had come down—promulgated. Bob and "Cannonball" sat themselves down at our table, ordered cups of coffee, and prepared to give us the facts. "Cannonball" carried the ball.

"Let us have, please, no misunderstandings," he began. He spoke carefully, meticulously, chose his English words slowly. "This musicale, jam session you call it, between the visiting American jazz musicians and some selected Russian musicians

addicted to playing western, jazz-type music is hereby author-
ized.

"Most important," continued "Cannonball," "this musicale
must take place in the afternoon, not in the night after the
concert or in the early hours of the morning. Understood? In
Russia people have to get up early in the morning and go to
work. This isn't America.

"A room in the ice rink is to be reserved for the event.
Programmed, too, is a bus to transport the participating musicians and bring them back to this hotel when the event is over."

"Fantastic!" cried Thad, when he heard the jam session was
okayed. It wasn't exactly what he had in mind—he'd never been
to a jam session in the afternoon, in daylight. Jazz needs the
night, but it was better than nothing. He rose, embraced Bob
and grabbed "Cannonball's" hand. "You're a beautiful cat," he
cried.

There were a dozen Russian musicians waiting for us when,
our breakfast over, we walked into the lobby. When the Russian
musicians heard there was to be a jam session at three P.M. that
afternoon, those who didn't have their instruments with them
hurried home to get them. It had never entered their minds that
such a wonderful, unprecedented event could happen to them,
playing jazz live with American jazz musicians in Russia.

I bought some rubles from the lady at the desk; then Thad
walked me over to the lobby gift shop. We ordered two bottles of
vodka, a pound tin of caviar, six packages of crackers, some paper
cups, and a spoon. "That should do it," said Thad.

Our sightseeing tour scheduled for that afternoon having been
postponed, we hung around the lobby of the hotel, waiting for
the Russian musicians to show up. We'd been there maybe half
an hour when Thad spotted those two brothers from Vilna and
that young cat on his way to Israel. "They're not musicians, but
hell, I'm going to invite them anyway," said Thad. "A jam
session's got to have an audience. And here's the chick from
Tbilisi. I got to hear her do that one jazz number in her
repertoire before I leave Russia."

"What about that nice Intourist lady who sits next to me on the
sight-seeing bus?" I asked Thad. "She wants to come."

"Let her," he cried. "Like we say at home: There's always
room for one more."

It occurred to me that maybe Thad was giving the jam session greater scope than was envisaged by the Russian Department of Cultural Affairs. But I didn't stop him, nor could I have stopped him if I tried.

"*Payakile!*" cried Cass as we boarded the bus.

When the crowded bus bearing us, the Russian musicians, and the guests Thad had invited—all in a festive mood—arrived at the ice rink, we found two cops standing at the entrance and two more cops in a jeep, waiting for us.

"Something's up," Bob said. "These aren't ordinary cops; they're from headquarters. One's a lieutenant colonel of police, and if the Russians send out a lieutenant colonel, it's got to be something important."

Eyeing us carefully, one cop opened the door of the ice rink to let us through. He was letting *us,* the Americans, through. The Russians, he shooed to one side: "*Nyet!*"

"What the hell's going on?" asked Thad.

We were inside and could see the Russians through the glass door, standing forlornly on the outside.

The director, a heavyset, well-barbered man, came over to greet us. He addressed Bob in Russian; Bob could handle him. We'd heard Bob talk Russian to the Russians before, but never so fast. We watched his pale face, not understanding a word.

"What's up?" Thad asked.

"No jam session, that's what's up," said Bob.

"You're kidding!"

"The director's a nice guy, but it's out of his hands. He got a phone call. He's gone upstairs to make another phone call."

The director, pale, worried, returned immediately and resumed his dialogue with Bob, who let us have it in English. "We can use the facilities of this facility this afternoon," said the director, "indeed, any afternoon during our stay in Leningrad, but not so the Russian musicians, he is sorry to say, nor the other guests Mr. Jones had invited."

"We ain't gonna use the facilities of this facility without the Russians," said Thad.

"This—how do you call it?—jam session, has taken on an unforeseen dimension. It has grown to unacceptable proportions and may prove an embarrassment, have some serious consequences, who can tell? The verdict has come down: better it be postponed," the director said.

"There's nothing more I can say," the director said turning to us, this time in English. "It is out of my hands. Maybe I should make another phone call? Yes?"

"Let's split, men," said Thad.

"*Payakile!*" cried Cass as our men moved to the bus.

"But first I've got to stop and apologize to the Russians," said Thad.

We were sitting in the half-empty bus, silent and brooding, waiting for Thad to apologize to the Russians. We could see him through the bus windows. Somebody broke open a bottle of vodka, took a swig, and passed it to the next man.

Thad's sure taking a long time, I thought. What could he be saying to the Russians? And what's he doing with his trumpet out of his case? A nice time to be showing off his trumpet to the Russians while we're sitting here waiting for him.

Suddenly we hear the sound of a trumpet, or is it a bugle, followed by a string of fast riffs.

"What's that?" said Cass.

"The key of C," said Mel.

"Max, please go get him," Bob said as if I had some authority over Thad.

I didn't move. Let Thad find his own way to the bus, I decided.

It wasn't five minutes before we heard Thad's footsteps on the gravel and saw his face at the bus door. He looked grim.

"What happened?" came hurtling at him from every corner of the bus as he sat himself down next to me. The driver started up the bus, and we were off.

Thad sat in silence for a few blocks. "They arrested one of them," he finally said. "The cop took his name down in his little black book and sent him home. How d'you like that?"

"Arrested him? What for? Blowing your trumpet?"

"I blew my trumpet."

"Hooliganism—he *let* you blow it—Right?"

Thad took a long swig out of the vodka bottle and passed it to me. "I don't know, I don't know why they arrested him." Then, turning to me, he said, "You're a smart sonofabitch. Why did they arrest that cat, and why wouldn't they let 'em go back in the bus with us? Why'd they say yes then no to the jam session? Why?"

"Looks to me like they don't want you messin' around with their men, Thaddeus Jones—that's what it looks like to me," I said as if I knew what I was talking about.

That night after the concert, Thad and I decided to take a walk. The hotel doorman gave us a suspicious look as we passed through the door. We walked a block and noticed some cabs parked in front of a dark door that kept opening and closing, letting people out and letting other people in. We walked in. The place was jammed. There was a bar. We sat down and ordered Scotch, for which we could pay only with dollars. We had two drinks each, walked out and back to the hotel.

It was still too early to go to bed, but since there was nothing better to do, we decided to call it a night.

"I still don't know what happened," said Thad. "The Russians are beautiful cats, but I don't get 'em." He held out the palm of his hand for me to slap, a characteristic gesture jazzmen have when reaching an impasse or coming to a conclusion.

Although we found it was true that you can't invite a Russian to dinner in Russia, and can't expect him to invite you to his house, nevertheless, it happened to me. The middle-aged Russian Intourist lady who went with us on the bus that took us on daily tours of Leningrad invited me for coffee and cake to her apartment, which she shared with her brother, a pianist. I said I'd be delighted to come.

Since she barely spoke English and I couldn't speak any Russian, she relayed her invitation to me through Woody, our second State Department aide. (We had two.)

Woody and I traveled to her apartment by the city bus. Fare— 4 kopecks which you dropped in a glass box at the entrance. You didn't have to; nobody watched you. They've got the honor system on buses in Russia—how do you like that? But if you didn't drop your kopecks the Russians called you a "rabbit."

"Why a rabbit?" I asked. Woody didn't know.

When we arrived at her small, three-room apartment, the table was set, the coffee on the fire, and a plate of sugared buns waiting on the center of the white table-cloth.

I saw a Bechstein piano in the next room. Her brother was on tour in Bessarabia, she told Woody who told me as we sat down and she commenced to pour the coffee.

I noticed a poster on one wall—a colored poster of four dancing male figures in leotards, "Les Freres Jacques," scripted across in large letters. I looked again to make sure. I have the very same poster on a wall in my apartment in New York—"Les Freres Jacques," a singing, dancing act that worked at The Blue Angel thirty years ago. They'd made me a present of one.

"What's the Russian word for 'fantastic?'" I asked Woody.

"And they worked for you thirty years ago in New York? How strange!" she said.

"They come here from Paris every year for concerts. They never fail to call on me. We are friends. We have coffee together."

"Yes, indeed, the personnel changes," she said sadly. "Every few years there's a new face. But they're still the same "Les Freres Jacques" and their material is still by the poet Jacques Prevert."

She waited for Woody to translate her words, a smile playing on her face as she listened and waited to see the effects her words were having on me.

"Why don't you come to New York one day?" I said suddenly.

"That would be, like you say, 'fantastic.' But," she added sadly, "rather impossible."

I didn't need Woody's help to get her meaning.

19 : Live at the Village Vanguard

It was the same every night when we were closing at 4 A.M.
There were always a few insomniacs and night prowlers left in
the place who never wanted to go home. Somewhere for a bite,
for a nightcap, anywhere, just to sit around and talk, and wear
away the morning hours while New York was asleep.

I too never wanted to go home; it was my only social life.
Besides, where was home? A furnished room on West Twelfth
Street. When I was getting started at the Vanguard, I used to
move every six months to another furnished room in the Village.
It wasn't until 1947 that I married Lorraine and moved to East
Ninety-fourth Street. Then I had a place to go home to. I'd get
home in time for my daughter Rebecca's 4 A.M. bottle. But all
that was later.

In 1941 Burl Ives was at the Vanguard. Then there were places
in New York that aren't around anymore. Lindy's is closed; the
Reuben's I knew is gone, and the Stage Delicatessen closes early.
It doesn't matter now—I couldn't eat a hot pastrami sandwich
with mustard at five in the morning if I tried. I remember
mornings when I could. We'd grab a cab to Reuben's on Fifty-
ninth Street, too late for a drink but in time for a sandwich. I
remember Burl gorging himself on one of the massive steak
tartars with onions they served there. After finishing one he'd
order another. I'd sit there goggle-eyed at his appetite. He was
living in a houseboat on the East River, so when we left
Reuben's, I'd let him take the first cab in the line.

Then I'd take a cab up to Harlem to Dickie Wells's all-night
joint, where they knew me. I couldn't drink the Scotch they
served, but there was always a girl who could. Before you knew

it, it was 7 A.M. In the streets in the grey morning air, you could see men hurrying into subways on the way to work, carrying their lunches in brown paper bags. I'd hail a cab and stop to buy a *Morning World*. I'd get into bed and lose more sleep reading Heywood Broun's column.

If it wasn't for a sandwich at Reuben's, it was for scrambled eggs at Lindy's. And we'd end up at the Howdy Club when it was still on West Tenth Street next to the firehouse.

It never failed but that somebody in the party would come up with the same two questions: How'd you get into this business? How've you kept going all these years?

I often get calls from undergraduates working on term papers, students from colleges where they offer courses in the history of jazz taught by professors of jazz, some of whom used to play jazz at the Vanguard only a few years ago. Some still do when their academic duties allow them—summers or during the Christmas holidays they take a gig in order to keep sharp on their instruments and earn a few extra bucks.

Their students want to see me and ask me some questions. "Your joint's history, man."

So they come down armed with cassette recorders and start asking me questions. Their opening question invariably is: How did you manage to keep it going all the years?

"Brothers and sisters," I tell them, "that's the story of my life. You haven't got the time, I haven't got the time, to plough up that much history in an afternoon. Ask me something simple, nothing so all-embracing, if that's all right with you. Remember I'm still at it, still running this joint, still trying to find the answers."

One senior from Rutgers College, a pretty, eager, self-confident girl adjusted her cassette for a fresh start and gave me a come ahead smile. "Relax, darling," she said. "You don't have to start at the beginning with me. I've been coming to the Vanguard for years. You haven't noticed me, but I've seen you standing around, doing what you're doing. I'd ask myself, 'Doesn't he ever take a night off?'"

"I'm here every night, needed or not," I said.

"Do you really enjoy it every night?"

"Running the Vanguard isn't all worry and trouble," I assured her. "If I walk in and the show is on, and I find a good crowd, that the men in the band have been on time that night, the lights are right and the sound level of the music is right, and nobody is hassling Jerry, the cashier, at the door, that the air conditioner is working and the ice machine's giving ice, and the new kitchen man isn't asleep in a chair like he sometimes is, I don't feel any pain—no pain at all—running the Vanguard that night."

"Have you ever had any real tough moments, running the place? I mean tough?" she asked me, still smiling.

"The night in the late thirties a Con Edison man walked in with a bill and a summons, and a cop to help him serve it—that was a tough moment. They pulled out the gas and electric meters and left the Vanguard in complete darkness. I thought I was through."

"So what did you do?"

"I operated by candlelight that night. Borrowed a hundred bucks from my sister the next day, paid the bill, and I was in business again.

"There've been other tough nights," I said. "The night I spent in the Charles Street police station, for instance. An irate customer had written a letter to the mayor complaining of the obscene graffiti, rhymed and unrhymed, on the walls of the men's room. I hadn't noticed it. The cop who came down to make the inspection informed me that tolerating—indeed, encouraging such obscenities as the letter proclaimed (he showed me the letter)—was a serious offense. 'You are therefore under arrest,' said the cop sadly.

"At nine that morning I was transported to the Jefferson Market court in a paddy wagon. The judge listened to the testimony of the arresting officer, and after giving me a close look, announced his verdict.

"'I don't believe,' the judge said, 'that the resident poets of this establishment have written these regrettable smudges on the walls of the men's room in order to enhance the business thereof, like this complaining letter claims. Let me give you a little advice,' said the judge. 'Keep a bucket of paint and a brush handy at all times. That's how to run a nightclub in Greenwich Village. Dismissed.'

"If only I could remember the name of that judge. I'd like to find him, shake his hand. He was a great judge. He could've thrown the book at me."

"So the years have piled up and here you are, still running your place every night like you used to?"

"No, not like I used to. I don't stay to the bitter end. I used to get to bed at 7 A.M. Now I'm up at 7 A.M., have breakfast after I'm up, not before going to bed like I used to."

"When, if ever, did you get mad at the Vanguard?" she asked. "I mean, when did you ever regret you opened the place?"

That was easy to answer. "On the days Elton didn't show up."

"Who's Elton?"

"Elton was the cook, dishwasher, porter, kitchen man—worked in the place for thirty years. When he didn't show up because he was either mugged or lost in some Harlem bar drunk, that's when I'd get real sore at the Vanguard.

"I'd roll up my sleeves, drag out the broom, mop, and pail and proceed to sweep, wipe, and wash the Vanguard clean—put it together again for the night's business. Many's the night I had to do it.

"No, I didn't fire Elton. I didn't fire him because of the quality of his hamburgers. Musicians who have worked in the place and are between gigs still come around looking for Elton's hamburgers.

"'Man, what'd you put in those hamburgers?' I'd ask him, and he'd say, 'Meat, man, plenty of red meat.'

"Elton was a no-nonsense man. He got his start in the kitchen of a kosher restaurant in the Bronx. When he was feeling right, he'd cook up *kasha varnishkes* for the help, and rice pudding and gefilte fish.

"We don't serve hamburgers at the Vanguard anymore, not since Elton retired. He saved his money and retired last year. He still comes down to the place when he can make it. Walks into the kitchen, keeps his hat on, puts down his cane and walks over to the sink and starts washing glasses—to show the current glass washer how it's done. He lifts a glass up to the light to see what he doesn't want to see.

"'Man, this cat don't know how to wash glasses.'

"I explain to Elton that this cat is no glass washer, that he's going to be an engineer, like his father in San Diego, and is only washing glasses nights to eat and pay the tuition days at that engineering school out in Brooklyn.

"Elton isn't satisfied.

"'Let him be an engineer if he wants to. He can't wash glasses.' And he calls the cat over to the sink to demonstrate the honest way to wash a glass clean."

*　　*　　*

"When Charlie Mingus worked at the Vanguard, he'd come early so he could eat his dinner before the first set. Charlie'd bring his dinner with him. He didn't trust Elton's hamburger meat, so he'd bring two pounds of ground filet, which he'd extract from a leather shoulder bag he carried. After eating three or four mouthfuls raw, he'd hand the package to Elton. 'Touch a little fire to this, brother. And do you have any onions left in the place?'

"One night while Mingus was fumbling for his package of meat, out fell a purse-sized hatchet from his leather bag. 'What's that thing doing in Charlie's bag?' I asked Elton once Mingus was safely on the bandstand.

"'Didn't you know Charlie carries that thing in his bag?'

"'What's he want a hatchet for?'

"'I'm not about to go and ask him,' said Elton.

"Elton knew you didn't ask Charlie Mingus a question like that."

"So you've been here almost fifty years! Wow! You must be some powerful cat," said the pretty senior from Rutgers.

"You're a beautiful young lady," said I.

"Take it easy," said she.

"Will you have something to drink?" said I.

"A glass of white wine," she said, "if you don't ask me to have another."

"When do you graduate?" I asked her.

"When I'm through asking you questions. This is my graduation thesis."

"Ask me any question you like," I said.

"I have only one more question," she said, taking the first sip out of her wine glass, "and please forgive me for asking it: What would you do different if you had it to do all over again?"

"Keep a bucket of paint handy, like the judge of the Jefferson Market court said I should."

"I'm serious," she said.

"May I have a second glass of wine, even if you won't have another?"

She was a smart girl and I enjoyed talking to her.

"When you get up too early in the morning like I do, and it's quiet and you're alone, sister, you got time to think. And what do I often think about? I think about just that: What'd I do different if I had it to do over again? One thing I'd do different is never to give anybody the rough treatment I gave a couple of kids about a month ago.

"It was one of those Saturday nights at the Village Vanguard: the stairs full of people waiting to get in for the second show. Anyway, I'm at my usual station near the door, worrying over the turnover, when a kid walks over to me.

"'Are you the owner?' he said. 'We come here often. My girl wants to know, are you the owner? She wants to know, does the Vanguard have an owner?'

"The joint is jumping and here this kid comes up to me with a lot of stupid questions.

"'Yeh, I'm the owner, buster,' I said to the kid, 'I run this joint. Tell it to your girl. Tell her the Vanguard has an owner. What does she think it is, Town Hall?'

"He walked away as if he'd been hit.

"I watched him go back to his table. I noticed he and his girl weren't even drinking. Maybe they're not such fresh kids after all. Maybe she meant it. Maybe she wasn't cracking wise. I thought I'd seen her in the place before.

"Then I caught her embarrassed glance in my direction. I should've walked over to her, put my arm around her shoulder. 'Baby,' I should've said, 'I'm not the owner. You're right, the Vanguard's got no owner.' That's what I should've said to her. But I didn't."

"You're crazy," said my pretty interlocuter from Rutgers. "You're the owner. The Vanguard has an owner. Why would you say a thing like that to her?"

"Hell, let her go on thinking it's Town Hall, if that's what she's thinking. Does that answer your question?"

"No," said she.

"I'm not through yet," said I.

"After running a place for as many years as I have, you discover that your place takes on a life of its own after a while. You started it, you put your ideas into it, your hopes and your dreams. It's your baby, but now it's got a life of its own, and you better know it.

"Look around and see what's happening to the place you

started. Don't stand there and crow, 'It's mine! I'll do anything I want with it. I own this place,' like I said that night to the girl.

"Take it easy, watch it, heed it, abide by it, if necessary. Talk to the people, and let 'em talk to you. Maybe you'll pick up a new idea or two along the way."